Goddess Awareness

From The

Feminine Aspect,

Ascended Masters &

VRC

No part of this book, either in part or in whole, may be reproduced, transmitted or utilized in any form or by any means, electronic, photographic, or mechanical, including photocopying, recording, or by any information storage system, without written permission from the publisher, except for brief quotations embodied in literacy articles and reviews.

Copyright © 2012 VRC

All rights reserved.

ISBN: 0-9871826-0-9
ISBN-13: 978-0-9871826-0-9

DEDICATION

This book is dedicated to the miracle of creation, life and the Creator.

A book does not come about without inspiration and help, and in this I consider myself to be divinely blessed for help and guidance have been there in abundance from the most enlightened and compassionate of beings in Spirit.

The Goddess, the Sacred Feminine since early times has been the victim of neglect, mistreatment and misinformation.

The Ascended Masters who have contributed to this volume have in their lifetimes worked to protect truth and restoration of the Sacred Feminine; to reinstate her back to a respected position in history as equal and dearly loved by the Creator.

I have absolute reverence and love for these great beings of light and a deep respect for the accomplishments achieved in their lifetimes with efforts in aiding the enlightenment of mankind.

Ignorance and lack of truth has kept humanity locked into patterns of violence and male dominance, and it is my hope this book Goddess Awareness – From the Feminine Aspect and others will ease the historical misconceptions, and a new light shines into dark places.

In particular I thank my beloved family for their patience, love and understanding of the time taken to write, and to receive these gifts of inspirational messages from the Masters.

I thank my beloved friends in Spirit the Ascended Masters, Lord Melchizedek, Aphrodite, Jesus Christ, Leonardo da Vinci, Sandro Botticelli, Isaac Newton, and Martin Luther King Jn. and other Masters who have been a constant source of wisdom, support, love and truth.

To these great souls I say thank you for your reverent love and support of the Sacred Feminine. I thank you for the courage displayed in your lifetimes speaking out, defending truth in every way to remove ignorance, and to shine the light of knowledge so that the consciousness of man may expand.

As humanity we have a long way to go to evolve out of ignorance and limitation of thoughts, but with your generous help and that of the Goddess and Ascended Masters we will make it.

In the name of the Goddess I thank you also, all those brave evolved souls on earth who chose to incarnate now at this most momentous of times.

To all of you who love Mother Earth as I do, and support truth and honour the feminine I send my deep and abiding love.

VRC

CONTENTS

	Foreword	1
	Welcome to Goddess Awareness-	
1	**The Return of the Goddess**	3
	Aphrodite-Power Restored	3
	Aphrodite – A New Light	6
	The Heavens Cry Out	10
	The Day Aphrodite Came Out To Play.	14
	The Feminine Steps Up.	19
	From The Feminine Perspective	24
2	**From The Feminine Aspect**	29
	Science Versus Religion	29
	Pakistan- Ease Their Pain	34
	Helios & Vesta	39
	Compassion	47
	Eternal Love	50
	We Are Star Stuff	53

	Peace Talks	57
	Know Thyself	62
	The Price of Love	68
	Heaven on Earth	71
	Planetary Alignment	75
	Defend God's Light	77
	Australia A Land of Hope	82
	Somalia – Global Upheaval	84
	A Mining Boom, After Boom Comes Bust – Gas Fracturing.	89
	America - A Plea - Support Barack Obama –	92
3	**Hope**	97
	The World Needs Hope	97
	Hope Starts With You	101
	Hope Mission Statement	104
	Hope - The New Energy	110
4	**Oneness**	117
	The Higher Teachings of Jesus	117
	Forgive Them Father	122

	Oneness - Return of the Flock	127
5	**Isaac Newton**	133
	Discrimination Against the Environment	137
	A Reflection Upon The Sacred Feminine	142
	In Defense of the Sacred Feminine	149
6	**Leonardo da Vinci**	155
	The Coming Gift of Love	155
	Truth & Liberation - Human	159
	Mona Lisa & Fundamentalism	163
	Ego	169
	Last Supper	174
	A Wakeup Call - Children -	180
	Oh Wretched Mortals	184
	The Pursuit of Truth	188
	The Ultimate Gift of Love	193
7	**Martin Luther King Jn.**	197
	Social Etiquette Versus Truth	197
8	**Sandro Botticelli**	203

	World Economic Recovery	203
	Religion - Has It Had It's Day?	207
	On Fundamentalism	212
	Truth	215
	The Evolution of Man.	220
	A Noted View of God	223
9	**Lord Melchizedek**	227
	The Lost Word	227
	Metatronic Keys	236
	Optimism Softens Hard Times.	240
10	**The Sacred Feminine**	243
	A Plea – Return Sacred Feminine ..	243
	From the Gentle Love of a Child	251
	Dragonflies – Breakers of Illusion	256
	An Invitation	261

FOREWORD

WELCOME TO GODDESS AWARENESS – FROM THE FEMININE ASPECT

When given a choice the very notion of one's worth is not something taken into account, but in this time of great striving for humanity, vast changes, and exemplary attempts to lift the human consciousness I see a need to propel forward the balanced view. Feminine energies are needed to bring balance back, and in Goddess Awareness I place my complete faith and hope.

It is my wish the feminine aspect bring through those views from the balanced energies of love, and it is with great joy do I say - Behold the Feminine Aspect; a new light to shine!

With love all can be healed, to many upon the human path new insights will come; a revelation they too are of divine heritage, and this awareness propel humanity forward at an unprecedented rate.

It is with my blessings Virginia writes, and it is with great pride I say, I now see balance being restored, that of the Sacred Feminine, so all beings find that lost element - lost to the passages of time and patriarchal oppression.

We welcome you, and bid you to see you are divine!

Lord Melchizedek.
Eternal Lord of Light.

ABOUT THIS BOOK.

Within this book there is a common theme, love and a return to balance and the need for the Sacred Feminine to be honoured and returned to her sacred place at the side of God.

This aspect to me is the most distressing that the Creator has been denied the feminine aspect; a main component of God's love is denied so an illusion can be kept of the supremacy of man.

This book is like no other for it contains guidance for living in the physical world from the Feminine Aspect and Ascended Masters who have devoted their lives to truth and the restoration of the feminine to her place of honour.

This is the ultimate book of love.

Virginia

The messages in this book are excerpts from Goddess Awareness website – a website dedicated to truth and restoring power to the feminine; and thereby aiding the raising of consciousness so humanity may evolve beyond ignorance and masculine dominance.

1 THE RETURN OF THE GODDESS

APHRODITE –
POWER RESTORED.

Challenges aside, deep respect comes for all enlightened souls, those who have had the courage to look within and structure lives based upon higher principles and awareness; awareness of global responsibility as citizens for this globe called Earth, and as divine creator beings for an awareness of the ability to shift the masses. For when one grows in vibration - a higher frequency, one also lifts others as a matter of daily awareness and conscious effort.

I am writing this through my beloved scribe, for this day does a new awareness dawn - a new vibration begins its steady flow into the hearts and minds of all beings. What does it do to gain the world if one's soul is not honoured in the process, and today marks the day of separation in real terms from love over fear, a battle continues across the globe, a battle for freedom, and this battle will continue well beyond 2012, because the level of awareness has now reached such a level as to sort those coming from love as opposed to fear. The barriers fall now, and a new level of excitement continues to enter the hearts and minds of people to aid the planet.

Why is today so very important? The full impact of the Goddess can be felt now as this loving energy flows out to soften hardened attitudes, to dissolve the overly masculine dominance and preoccupation with aggression and war, and an especially glorious event takes place. A grace is given to planet earth to aid her, and Aphrodite in all of her aspects now holds this magnificent planet safely in the energy of love, to enable her to progress in her own restructuring, but I must add here; any area of heavy war like attitudes, any lands which harbour masculine suppression of the feminine will now feel the full impact of her power.

Aphrodite some may say 'Goddess of Love, she is but a temptress, a lover, and not of real power', but can I tell you about Aphrodite - Venus, she is real, and she holds this planet now in a safe space for her progression into the ascension energies. Aphrodite is not as told in your fables, she is divinely inspired to show love as the feminine aspect of God; there are many stories of the feminine aspect now, none of which show the real power and beauty of her love. Not a wishy-washy energy so to speak, but a love so strong it can sustain, but also dispel and reduce to nothing negativity in any form, so if I sound as if I am in awe of the energies of Venus – Aphrodite, it is because I am. Complete respect I have for the raw power of her energy to dispel heavy energies, to dissolve darkness, and to heal with love situations which previously seemed not to have a solution, and by the power of her love this next phase of planetary healing and cleansing comes.

To some this may sound ridiculous that the feminine is the ultimate dissolver of darkness, but can I explain? Fear, anger, war like tendencies all rely upon one thing for fear to hold power, and love is seldom present with heavily infested areas of male aggression and dominance.

All over this planet and beyond a softening comes, a sweet energy to disarm and soften, and make no mistake this energy will sustain you if the heart is open, and sustain Mother Earth herself. So I do pay homage to Aphrodite - Venus now, and say to her you are honoured, we who support planet earth and all of creation work with you to bring about change.

Planetary changes come now gently, quietly for some, but rapidly for others who in their desperation ask for help, and her energy now pours forth upon all life. Sweetness will enter the domain of politics across the world, and diplomacy strengthens, and any signs of aggression will be dispelled.

To fight the power of love is not possible, because it flows from her directly from the sacred heart of God. Oh children of the earth, your divine nature will now be shown to those open to it, and a wisp of light enters the heart, but be prepared to share your love with each other and with Mother Earth as she cleanses herself of those aspects and areas of the heaviest negative buildup.

We love all beings, all life, but on planet earth there has been such an imbalance of masculine energy as to cause destruction on a massive scale. So see this as my need now, that an understanding comes this day, Venus - Aphrodite delivers her love now to all of creation to redress any imbalances, and in her hair she wears the crown of stars given at her birth, and on her hand she has a bird sitting, and blows a kiss and says, "spread your wings gentle creature, fly to all lands, to all places not seen, and say in the soft flutter of your wings I am come. I am come unto this creation project to interject, to counter wrong use of power, and to say, behold the Kingdom of God is within," therein is her energy sent forth, to caste out fear in the darkest of places.

From today expect climate events to grow in intensity and duration, until there is an awareness of the beauty and power of the feminine and total honouring of Mother Earth, and by that I mean there is a responsibility taken by all nations across the board to reduce damage to Mother Earth's survival mechanisms. Mother Earth enters this period now of heavy reduction of pollution, a reminder of responsibility all need to take.

Love can heal the situation, but it is of your making and will need a rapid change of attitudes now. You can do this; you have all the help you need. Awareness of your heritage now flows, so it too your legacy, one which has ability to change; that of polluters of Mother Earth to her saviours.

All will flow now with a gentle awareness, hatred and anger, all lower energies are now to be counteracted by the power of the feminine, and she will have our help to shift humanity and all life into the new age of love.

Blessings.
Lord Melchizedek.

APHRODITE - A NEW LIGHT.

From the Sacred Feminine comes a new light, an energy enhancing light, and a given placement in honour at the right hand of God. Until now all pre-assigned roles as extension beings to download Gods light have come in masculine form, or in an image of a masculine form.

Given that all ascended beings have fully integrated both masculine and feminine aspects and perform functions as a male prototype or female aspect; we will now state that the delineated light now streaming forth from God is balanced energy, but now emphasis is placed upon the feminine being restored to a position of publicly holding an energy for the Creator to bring balance back to creation on earth and elsewhere across the cosmos; in any area where imbalance has gained a hold and where masculine aggressive energies now hold power.

It is in this capacity, I Aphrodite, or known to some as Venus do hold energy in place for love now to formulate this new direction, one with a dominant direction of installation of a new light stream and characteristic beam of energy into this planets energy placement system.

On occasions I will introduce a subject relevant to this discussion topic, and guide that general direction, but I will not as a feminine representative of the Supreme Council of Light and Great White Brotherhood and Sisterhood of Light dominate discussion points, but aid in new directional forms of communication.

In other worlds the prominence of masculine domination is not so pronounced as on this magnificent planet, one now in need of some care and restoration. There will be a new light in the heavens, one with a distinctive shade of blue, an optical illusion? No, and as etheric reconstruction and elevation of consciousness needs a corresponding light transformation; shades of blue will begin to develop a new shade, due in principle to an influx of subatomic particles and frequency bands of vibration oscillating at a new frequency.

Given that this new energy coincides with planetary reconstructing and refurbishment of Earths renewal and survival mechanisms I pour my energy, my frequency as a direct light from God given into incremental transformational energies, whereby that new light will shine and glow in the heavens, but also permeate all levels of strata and cell development of earth, and all creations within and upon the planet.

Over a period of fourteen months I will pour forth this new light frequency and coded language of light to all dimensions, and into the portal offshoots which filter broken down light in manageable forms. Of this time many speak of endings, of catastrophic events and portents, but few if any speak of the summoned call of my Father, Creator of all life to awaken to the fullness of being and come home.

The year 2012 is spoken of in terms of fear. Will the world end on December 21, 2012, or will it simply evolve, the world as you know it? Of this time I will say the Goddess, the Feminine Aspect of God will be active in restoration of the feminine, and through me, and other feminine forms of Masters, light, wisdom and grace will be shared with you; that you may find this time of critical transformation to be not only comfortable, but also aligning with your soul choice to come to earth at this time.

I along with others will read aloud a new call into the heavens – "One era is concluding, we call to all of creation, return home to the Creator, to God, and bring with you love of all creation as one!"

With a gentle set of journals* will we initiate those who are interested to come together and become the Light. Upon the first day of March 2012 a new energy will flow, noticeable to some and very penetrating of all tissues, composite energies and form. There will be a new framework for the creation of a new era of love, but a separation comes - one of fear from love.

No longer will unbalanced energies flow into areas of reform, planetary harmony will come by the compassionate response of individuals to planetary - environmental, political and social upheaval. A cleansing now takes place, and with this cleansing a new underlying understanding begins to grow of life as unbalanced. You will feel the love as increasing, you will see this transformative process continue, and visual will it be, as well as felt in physical form.

We grace you humanity with a new energy, that of increased love and feminine energies to clear out from the human component that problematic aggression and violence, but part of this cleansing will mean that a painful process comes, one which is now dormant in many countries.

In Bahrain, where women fight for the rights which should have flowed centuries ago we will penetrate all layers of society, of creation, and give to the very center of areas of trouble a new power; one which will not be stopped, not by intransigent attitudes of men and masculine dominance.

I speak now on behalf of all those Masters and Goddesses who work now to bring forward these times. Instead of speaking of years of cleansing, we say that the next fourteen months are the most critical to human evolution.

Love guides you, and love will be that dominant light.
Aphrodite

THE HEAVENS CRY OUT – HOPE COMES UPON THE WINGS OF LOVE.

Tomorrow is always a repository for the acts and deeds of today, but a gathering storm flows across the land, a motion not of love and gestures of goodwill, but fear, an angry energy so far from the loving gestures humanity can bestow upon creation. Around the world this gathering storm of fear manifests in attitudes, in politician's speeches, in fear driven discussions which impede forward growth; and the prolific growth which can flow when love is strongly within the thoughts and minds of aware people.

Around the world now there flows a fear gathering its mighty storm of agitation and anger as fear does; it closes down energies and at a time the world needs love most, this fear is now pulling down energies and gathering force.

Oh my children I speak now as Aphrodite Goddess of Love, and into your hearts do I pour my blessings that you may find love there strongly in all situations, and from this energy transformation as does flow from my heart to you now, do I also grace you with this understanding of the problematic times you are entering as not beyond your ability to transcend, to raise not only your own energy but all around you. Love that inescapable energy comforts you as you find your place of peace to negotiate the troubled spaces which come not as a trial to test you from some unseen God, but the combined efforts, of actions, thoughts, and deeds of all beings.

Mankind has the opportunity to ascend and take creation with you out of this fear dominated space, but onwards and upwards into a new dimensional reality; one of peace and beauty.

My words today are those of one who comforts you - all who feel at a loss to understand present day trends, downturned market economies and events to test the very mettle of your souls, but my children, love is with you, within you daily, in your every gesture of grace we uphold you in your times of great trial, but also we urge you to see your own potentials as creator beings.

As a whole, as humanity your realities are created daily, and the combined thoughts, acts and deeds are what your planet is experiencing now in combination – a true spiritual testing not by an angry God, but by your own souls. You have the ability to transcend all trials which come to you, but as part of creation, as an integrated linkage of energy of all events come, some which bring pain to millions of souls, some affect people, groups, countries or areas. At the moment millions of people, men, women and children, babies and animals are facing starvation, are now in dire straits and in need of assistance.

We could appeal to your better nature and urge you to aid others in whatever way you can, or we can say: you are starving, it is happening to you right now; be aware you are interlinked - interconnected with every other soul on this planet and beyond.

You are as part of your global body experiencing fierce droughts, pestilence and starvation, and in Pakistan starvation and homelessness from an entirely different manner of an excess of water, great floods - millions without homes, without the food and without uncontaminated water. It is your body which suffers, your child, or baby which lies lifeless without hope.

It is the greatest pain which is experienced now. This lack of connectedness now leaves many feeling this is part of the tragedy elsewhere and so best left forgotten, that if people experience this it is their karma. But my children you are that baby dying, you are that mother who watches her family die, for there is no separation. You are one with every living being, you have just forgotten who you are. Your divine heritage as sons and daughters of the Creator, you are one with everything, you laugh and cry and the world laugh and cries too. You by your very nature are love, it is what you were created from, and to love you will return, but on this earthly realm you created, a forgetfulness came of separation from God and each other.

While you allow another anywhere to suffer and close your hearts and minds this separation continues. Oh my beloveds love is all you are, in the beginning it is your very nature, and now I ask, I Command all of light and love to activate this remembrance pattern to awaken that dormant memory of love and explode in positive potential. See with a new vision of the world you create now from this point on as coming from compassion and joy.

Oh I Am Aphrodite and I do now beseech you to reach out in an awakened time of recreation; look at your world in a new light that you may know the joy of creation, a recreation of this world, one balanced, restored in love and dedication to make a difference, to see the potential for positive change and make it happen. In a new wave of joyous celebration of life join with others to create groups, movements of hope, make your life count! Be the hero you could look up to, and where there is fear instill love and balance, compassion given to any raises the energies of the whole.

So many have seen this time only from the viewpoint of fear, and overlook potential for positive change; and the greatest gift that can be given now is to love life enough to stop this flow of negativity and fear driven closing down energies of compassion. Raise funds for those in need, devote your life not to chasing wealth and economic boom, but love, and creation of a world devoted to principles of inclusion, to love, and healing those areas of greatest pain.

We know it seems insurmountable when confronted with images full of victims of floods, drought and violence, how easy it is to close down and shut the mind and heart, and join those so closed they dig into protectionism, the exclusion of others, and denial of aid where needed.

This is a planet of plenty, and around your world there is a blessed plenty which can be shared, given to those in need to aid them through situations which seem insurmountable. It is my greatest gift to share love, and to those in pain I Aphrodite pour out to you my love and blessings, but I also remind you of your divine heritage, and ask you to take that leap of faith in the future and reach out to help anyone in need. It is through love humanity overcomes some of these trials; all manmade.

It is with love and compassionate understanding we, all who represent God's Kingdom, call you to attention and say; set a new standard and raise it high that love and hope transcend fear; and transmutes negativity, thereby raising energies at a most appropriate time. Karma may have been called for in some areas, but is it not also an act of compassion to reach out and help others shift any heavy accumulation of energies by importing compassion and love in acts of kindness? To give food, water, tents, blankets and clothing, these are the acts of a divine being, one awakening from the slumber of separation, bringing to all a new way of life called hope - one movement of love all can join and pay it forward, and such is so needed now.

Of all those gestures of love given now, let your love of the Creator and creation be restored.
Come home to love my beloveds, we miss you; this separation has lasted too long.

A gentle movement of love can come with the first action you take to do good, and impart higher energies; then this is heaven on earth.

It is my summons now I give to all of creation, love calls to all beings; be awakened now, surrender forgetfulness, and offer love to all. This we do give now in sublime offering to you Oh humanity that you may experience love as we do. Be the gift of gentle winds which sweep away despair and pain, lift the human condition and do it now in my Father's/Mothers blessed name.

Advance; go forward with love in your heart. I cast out all darkness that does dull the Light and say; Oh holly messengers of Light awaken that dimensional portal through which only love may pass. It has come to pass; the very nature of goodness and compassion is now set free, come fly with me upon the gentle winds of change - that empowered by love.
Aphrodite.

THE DAY APHRODITE CAME OUT TO PLAY.

What is the advantage of love over hate? Love brings joy and a playful energy with it. Aphrodite, Goddess of love, spoken of for so long as temptress brings to humanity now a new energy of hope. Not an energy of pleading and holding on so tenaciously to fear of what might occur, what life can stir up, but bring to all now a playful resolve that all is perfect, will be perfect, because love is there as the principle energy of world practice.

It does little good to promote a way forward dominated by fearful thoughts of what may come, instead the energy she brings through now to all of creation is her Father's love, a love so deep, so divine, the hardest of beings start to mellow and soften, and into the consciousness of all human beings now she pours forth the healing waters of Hope. Hope not as a plea to the universe and God, as powerless beings do when not standing in full power, but the joyful response of gratitude for every small gesture of goodness and love shown - gratitude for daily events and love being shared with others. Love the inescapable energy of the exploration of goodness shown begins to filter into the consciousness of man. No area of life will be exempt now from hope, it is no longer just a word, but is now a living breathing energy, breathed into every creation capable of sustaining life.

Love will no longer be an expectation only of what one obtains, but the joy also of experiencing an outpouring of energy from every sentient being capable of sustaining joy.

Oh, life for many people will bring to them hard times, but perceptions change as life will change, and hope being the foundation stone for a New Jerusalem flows, but not a solid structure to build upon as a Mason does when conceiving and building a new concept of structural design. This hope as a cornerstone will be the platform upon which life now functions, in that the expectations are no longer for the self alone, selfish attitudes begin to dissolve, and structure now takes form of love as solid, concrete in every way because it paves the way for better human relationships.

Hope is now not a plea to a distant God for help, but a filtering recognition taking form that each and every one of us are God, of God, and therefore powerful in the extreme. Each and every soul has now has the capacity to issue love and hope out - in conceptions of concrete actions, helping others, seeing the state of the world and saying. "Let us be the hope others need. Where food and shelter is needed we can do this."

It shouldn't be we as humanity wait upon God for a wish, a prayer to come true. It is time to accept our power, each and every one of us and say. "I love my life because I am not separate to others, I am not isolated from that child starving in Somalia, my every act of kindness anywhere upon the planet begins energy flowing, and as a concrete act of generosity and kindness we become the sculptors of a new reality". No longer do we give our power away and wait upon the universe or God to do it for us, and God does love us, but we were also given divine power to create or destroy, and it's done every day with extremes at times, but joyful recognition and awareness of our every action begins this expressive movement of hope, and the world becomes a more peaceful, powerful place where individuals learn finally to live life fully balanced and empowered.

No longer are we the victims, but we become the creators, far more powerful and beautiful. What joy does when included in action is to increase the intensity of the actions, joy speeds the delivery of positive action, and when we find joy in becoming something greater, we share joy and love with others.

Of the coming times I have been shown at a great deal. Over the next twelve years vast changes come, those some would describe as catastrophic, and Lord Melchizedek has issued be with words and visions. I could say we face some problematic periods of experience, but instead I will just say now, that we are blessed to live in the most powerful time in human history, to shift, move and 'become'. We have all the divine help we need, but to await such periods with despair and a sense of hopelessness and powerlessness decries our divine heritage. We are as humanity made of something greater, we are the shape shifters, the gentle ones, those with integrity and purity of nature, we were born to be sculptors of a new reality - one which empowers creation, and not to be seen by far off worlds as the pariah, that race who let selfishness and greed overcome the divine nature.

Oh my way is now given, to act as a guide to help you remember who you truly are, a miraculous mover of mountain's, the creator of a world where war like tendencies are denied, and put aside as one does a child's toy when no longer needed, and seen from a higher viewpoint.

When Lord Melchizedek handed me this baton to run with in his times of absence from message giving for this website, he said! "My dove, it is time you saw who you are, and in your power remind others who they are, and do it your way. I handed you this baton now, as we, the masculine aspect of the Spiritual Hierarchy have run enough races to know that we do not give what is needed now, feminine aspect and insights - the world viewed from a gentle aspect of love. But speak truth my dove, and spare no one that truth needed, but how you do this I cannot now decree.

The feminine is needed, and the energy you give compliments mine now. When necessary I will still come to deliver words, but until you strike out in the name of love I will hold back. My words have power in them, but yours have equal power, you just deliver them your own way." To this I said at that time, Oh my Lord, people do not want my words, it is yours that are needed, but over time I have learned he never wasted a word, never! Always he has been so very right about issues and subjects we have spoken about, and always did I come around to see his words had truth, it was just my perceptions and lack of understanding at a time which clouded my judgment. I now see the truth in his words, the feminine is sadly lacking in this world of conflict, and a sense of dread and fear pervades headlines, people fear.

This then is my introductory note that it is time the feminine reclaimed her power, and softly, silently to a point, project out now love, joy, and hope into the hearts of all beings.

Love is not powerless, but powerful beyond all measure, and nothing can deter the feminine when love is needed, and this world now experiences the love of Aphrodite pouring forth, each and every day, every moment, and time and space now flows with this energy. It is a gift from the Creator that love is given to caress the senses, to soften angry words, and to open hearts, and where the human capacity to change war like ways is slow to mold to a new way, love will bring that peace and understanding on some level. So no one is exempt, a circumstance may come where situations challenge, but the hope we incorporate in the form of love can aid, sooth and soften.

Hope is a nourished view of life that we are not a singular beings, but part of a much greater, larger family, the brotherhood and sisterhood of mankind. Where the next twelve years takes us is very much up to us. We are the creator beings who say "let there be light, let hope be given to all souls, it is the ultimate expression of love from God, Creator of all there is!"

What it takes to shift humanity is a deeper understanding that we are one essence issuing from God, and therein is truth. Love will set us free, love, and joy and hope we create daily as an expression of our soul needs to honour all life.

No one can escape the subtle energies of Aphrodite, she pours her love out, and the feminine now restores and holds this magnificent planet in a space she can also be transformed and empowered.

I will not say all will change and rapidly, this is not possible, as love flows, so hatred and fear is metered out to cancel out such powerful energies of love, but there is no power stronger than love.

We (*as humanity*) are what we have waited for! We are those powerful beings who in a moment of realization say, I am more, and love enters, and the impact flows on like a seismic wave, it flows out entering every pore, every cell and thought.

Only love can save this magnificent planet, but will we, that is the question? All is provided for us, all preparations made for this time by the Spiritual Hierarchy, but will we awaken?

I do see this as strongly there now because love flows, and so it is a new day begins that femininity is restored, but also a realization love is not powerless, love is divine.

Blessings.
Virginia.

THE FEMININE STEPS UP.

A strengthened view of life comes now to all those open to love and energies now being beamed to you humanity, but it would take a gift of great love to heal this world and move it into a new light of understanding. We have offered you guidance in this website for many years, but over the coming two years vast changes will come, potential breaks to your communications, and static breaks, of solar winds, solar activity, whereby some disruption also comes to all Internet & telecommunications Industries as well.

It may be some years away before the content of these words are valued, and a public note is made, "why didn't we value this earlier, if only we had known of this guidance and opportunity to look at the world around us and change it, but my beloveds this is a time to look to the next phase of our preparation to aid you, and we cannot give guidance to you in the future and not have our words also be obtainable by those who would misuse our words for their justification of actions not of love.

Your world now experiences changes, some subtle, some severe and not open to endorsement of change by humanity. A hardening takes place as the mind and heart is shut, and so less action is taken to protect this magnificent planet.

We who oversee humanity are with you every step of this journey, never are you alone, know that, but just as a child is gently taught and given guidance and help, and grows to a stage personal free will allows the lessons of life to come about, so too has humanity.

It is time beloveds you look globally now at your handiwork, and say; "yes this is the way we can contribute to life and healing this planet". We, that parental image must stand aside and say we have groomed you to a point. We have offered advice and nurtured you, and still do when you hurt yourself, but we have done all we can of advice, and I, Lord Melchizedek, Eternal Lord of Light and planetary Logos of Light now leave it to you to shape your world. As at that time of Melchizedek when I came to earth to teach of love and simple rules of life - to break the back of ignorance and need to hold to lesser values, to stop the sacrifice of truth, animals and people for human need for a masculine power, I now as then have reached a stage I must let you learn your lessons, and say you are co creators. You can make or break this world, and you can do it actively with knowledge we the Spiritual Hierarchy have tried to awaken you to your divinity and connection to God.

We, I, have tried to say 'change your ways', and although many have changed and continue to awaken, I can through my beloved partner not continue to offer words. There comes a point of time I need to say 'you are the masters of your own destiny'!

In the time of Melchizedek, or as Jesus Christ, or Akhenaton, or King David, I came with one purpose, but now I speak through the words and consciousness now of a woman to say 'be the light of generosity and understanding'. Become all you can be, and stop this madness and greed before it consumes you as humanity. We are here for you, and you have all you need. It is as I have said in my messages, all is prepared for the times ahead to aid you, guidance is there, and I have left my beloved partner to speak in my stead through the times to come, but be aware, I will not be coming to give words on a regular basis.

Your world is now in your hands! To those who would say 'why would he stop giving messages if times of becoming hard'? I simply say, you are the creators of your world, you are powerful and wonderful even as you are cruel and heartless in those times where fear dominates, and you are fully conscious beings who read these words. You are God's extensions on earth, you make all the difference! We love you humanity, but we love you enough to allow your free will to flow, and know what you do with life will be beautiful, or terrible, the choice is yours.

Like that proud father who watches and has groomed the beloved child, we stand back and say, Oh the choice is yours to become something so much greater, and grander, or the choice is to be less; and that is something some people do not understand. That karma is real, and good deeds come back, just as negative karma accumulates and impacts, but we love you anyway. Whatever you do we are here with you loving you, aiding you, but just as that parent sets a child upon the path of life, that same parent weeps when poor choices come.

I am Lord Machiventa Melchizedek and I hold you safe, your soul choice was to incarnate at this time to be part of a major production - the ascension of humanity, to become something greater, and we aid you with that.

We, I and my beloved partner have had just such a path where I nurtured her through very many years where she didn't see the value of a female, didn't have a powerful self image, and didn't see who she was; divine just as you are, and I like that very proud parent have watched at times, wept at her pain as she learned the world was more. I have smiled so many times when she overcame her fears and learned to love, and to see me not as her saviour, or a Lord of Light to place on a pedestal, but came a time she could challenge me, question me as an equal, and at that time I also wept, for I saw a glimpse of the future start to change. I witnessed a gift that would bring some joy, and to others pain, as an awakening took place, where femininity found its place in the world; not as a hard energy ready to do battle to achieve equality, but the softer energy of love began to move out across this world, healing, nurturing and loving.

I am Lord Melchizedek, Eternal Lord of Light, but I stand at a moment of joy for me to see my beloved partner finally accept who she is, and in that is joy for us all. Now that meek, downtrodden self image of the feminine as without power and a voice has gone, and in its place a woman who can take my words and deliver them without fear of what people may think, and this is also a great pain for in stepping back to allow her to grow stronger; I am not able to steer her course, just smile or frown as she finds her steps, shaky at first and then stronger.

Some would wonder why I speak of this evolving in this way, when I may still come to some around the world for a time, it is because to her do I give my words to comfort humanity and guide them. Oh yes I come to many, but to one do I give the hard words, the truth others would not find palatable or cost effective.

To her do I say, my dove; this day has come for you to move forward now as equal, show others they are divine, and of the same light. Share with them truth, and if in times of trial I am needed I will still come to give words, but this is now the time for the feminine to reclaim power, to seize this world with love and pour nurturing energy out to all life, and to Mother Earth herself.

This is time for the feminine to reclaim power, and a male image of a Lord of Light may carry the age old image of power and dominance, but it is now time for a change. The energies now given to aid humanity through these times are feminine, softer, subtle, but make no mistake tyrants will fall. Totalitarian regimes will begin to crumble, not under the weight of masculine dominance and power - a heavy handed fear based energy, simply the soft wind of change, one which flows into the most hardened of attitudes and hearts. Corrupt governments, oppressive governments, male dominated military regimes all feel weaker somehow, as if the very structure which holds them together begins to dissolve, and there is absolutely nothing that can be done to stop this!

It comes now as a soft wind of change from God that the little ones, the Creators little ones begin to remember love.

A male dominated Hierarchy, or an image of one is now not what we wish to promote. We wish to correct false illusions God is masculine and favours the male, so I Lord Melchizedek hand over the reins to the feminine to speak at times, or not, as she sees fit; and to restructure, reshape, and give hope to the world.

Wherever you are, in whatever country, you now will feel the impact of the feminine, and this is across the board, any dominant organisation or group, nation or person who feels they can hang onto power wrongly held be advised. God sends the feminine essence out across the cosmos, and it will not be stopped, and to fight to hold onto male domination will only intensify God's love and the feminine. Balance is needed, and needed so badly now!

I come today to my beloved partner to say, I set you free my dove, fly high and do not again see the feminine as less than a man. It is time for the goddess to spread her wings and say 'behold a new energy is here, come fly with me as equals'. No longer will we have imbalance, for that illusion of power held over time will fade. I give you the time of the feminine, one I defend, and say follow your own light of understanding, knowing so very many need help, show the world their own beauty, majesty and grace, and know I will always be there.

It is the day of grace being restored, that balance and God's counterpart the Feminine Aspect is restored to her place of honour, the ignorance of mankind cannot keep her trapped any longer. To the Feminine Aspect I bow and say; Ah at last God has the flocks returning to love, for love is all she is.
Profound Peace to you.
Lord Melchizedek.

FROM THE FEMININE PERSPECTIVE

The initial response to Lord Melchizedek's message was sadness, that a time with him coming to teach me has ended, that I will miss his influence, but also a feeling of recognition is there that the feminine so maligned and held hostage to man's whims has now an opportunity to 'become', worldwide to step up and reclaim power, and that overcomes my sadness of Lord Melchizedek not coming to teach me, groom me, or show me reflections of what human frailty can do. I have loved the many years he has guided the way, showing me at times the error of my ways, reflecting hard lessons, letting me see the beauty of people, seeing beyond the hard words and closed hearts; to see through his eyes, to see why people are so afraid - why we so often wear a mask and hide the real us.

Our world has evolved, and devolved in many ways, and never before have we had the opportunity to shift as now, but it isn't painless or easy. Love is what we have as a direct lifeline from God, love flows to us constantly; it is an open source energy available at no cost. All we need to do is to open the heart.

Someone said to me last night, "but it's hard, at the very time we need to have our heart open, one simple event or comment can have us crashing down, shutting the heart. How do we stop this trend and learn to love more". My comment; find your personal key to unlocking the heart, for some it is music, for others to sit in nature, but all is available to us constantly with an awareness of God, and I know the very mention of God has some people running for the hills, for the overtones of religion is heavy, not so. God is a concept we can't get our heads around, the very idea of such power we cannot fathom, added to that the concept of God or 'Creator' or 'The All' however you wish to describe God, love is all there is. This defies our ability to understand, but the intellect won't get us there with understanding of the magnificence of love.

I am blessed with knowing from my early childhood God was part of me, as also in a flower, a frog, or to sit and feel this energy and connectedness in nature. So the answer is for me personally to find something I truly love and appreciate, and then the magic happens, and ecstatic energy flows, divine, pure, and immeasurable, and the awareness is there we are supplied with an endless source of love constantly. It is there at every moment just by loving. I realise in war and a time of extreme trial fear enters, and then it is hard to hold the energy of love, but it's not impossible.

At this time I am saddened for Lord Melchizedek to hand the reins to me for this aspect of nurturing humanity, but I will not go into my feeling of inadequacy, for that negates the love and faith he and the Ascended Masters who have supported me have, instead I will say, I love life, love God and I know I have a gift to give, simple words perhaps but full of love.

Events will come I have been shown where our compassion is needed, where hope is needed, and that extends to animals and all life. We are not conquers of the earth as some religious leaders have told; that mankind has the right to dominate and conquer the earth. Perhaps the gift I can share is total love and appreciation for all life. I am intimidated by Lord Melchizedek's request, but I know truth is needed, and the softer words of a woman does not mean they have less power or potency in them. Sometimes love and gentleness has a way of caressing the hardened views of life easing the pain, and creating a gentle environment for change to take place.

The way of the feminine may be subtle, but not less powerful. Love can heal many of the world's woes, not all of them, they were created by mankind, and now the feminine can ease the way. It is my hope you will join us on this web site while it is still exists in cyberspace, it is here for you if you should need to hear truth through the feminine.

Love is the energy we hold for you to ease the days ahead, please join us.
Virginia.

2 FROM THE FEMININE ASPECT

SCIENCE VERSUS RELIGION

Advances in science have come so far, and with it an understanding of the principle pathways of neurology, chemistry, astrophysics and all manner of sciences, and science related topics, and globally we have come so far. We as a race have gone to the moon, observed the stars and sought the knowledge of the atom, and yet do we truly know our own world? A world of grace and interconnectedness of all species, that related topic now such a bone of contention with science vs. religion, and the closed view that it is all of one, and not an element of both.

In my studies I have found the inner relationship to matter is very much a part of science that can be measured and to some degree quantified. In these mystical studies I have been graced with some knowledge of ancient beliefs and customs of people, and also looked at the great philosophers, mystics and alchemists, and to some one cannot look at these subjects without ridicule from those limited numbers who believe that science of today cannot to be brought into mainstream thought because it cuts out God.

Oh I see this as a blindness that has long existed over time, where limitation of thought has very much been the happy option, because to allow freedom of thought and knowledge some believe corrupts, because of those long entrenched beliefs that the 'word' was written, and "it is so, and so it must be today" and my soul wants to cry out "awaken please".

Religion is the region of faith, and science is science, methodical practices or theories, tested and retested and proven by fact; where religion is faith held onto out of many beliefs and perceptions. I have seen the very nature of man described in such primitive terminology as to make me think, "why won't they give up this need to hold books, documents changed so many times there is little left of the original tenets behind it"?

Science and faith can be blended, and this many of the great thinkers, geniuses of the world have done and been persecuted for in years past, and to some extent still today.

Some would be horrified to think that I a mere female would dare to deliver Lord Melchizedek's, Master Luke's and the Great Masters words, or say I have felt Jesus Christ's energy and thoughts, but it's true, and one thing I can say, in all the time I have been working with Spirit, I have never ever believed that God was judgmental. Just the opposite!

I haven't heard one word which states that science has no place, or technology. We evolve as a race and where we take knowledge and skills is up to free will, but there is good reason to teach Charles Darwin's theories, because these have shown through competent research from some of the most respected and prominent scientists of the world, that the world is more than we were told, hundreds of years ago. It is limiting the human race to try to enforce a doctrine of creationism in schools, and try to make rational human beings teach what is not factual. Religion is based on faith, that does not mean that one can't keep one's faith in God, and still be open to scientific research.

My concern is when man sees himself/ herself as God and starts to use skills to alter the genetic code of plants, organisms and animals. The earth and creations upon it aren't here for human manipulation and control, and quantifying into resource base products, which may come back in years to come to haunt us. I believe we as evolving beings must move forward, but always question all theories and make some adaptations to change with time. I am writing of this, for is a great concern when reading of the fundamentalist religious groups who want to suppress human expression, and limit the human understanding of the greater universe, one of the countless universes in the cosmos because of closed ideas.

God is not limited energy, but unlimited, with compassion and understanding, and it saddens me that such pressure is exerted to squash down knowledge, because some people can't expand the mind and move forward with time.

Jesus Christ, Muhammad, Buddha, Krishna and all great enlightened beings had truth to share, and they would, and are saddened that some still hold to old energies with such fear of allowing knowledge out to others.

I am with Leonardo in this, "Oh retched mortals open your eyes!" but I would add a reminder. You cannot be harmed by allowing knowledge in, and others should not be held down by limiting beliefs which may have served some people in the distant past to hold onto to a semblance of power and righteousness.

Times have changed, but sadly there is still an element of that old energy around experienced at the time of the inquisition - suppression of freedom of thought. Dangerous this is. Why promulgate such fear of knowledge and ignorance in any form? Have faith in your own soul to guide you and keep you safe as you allow the walls around such fear to go.

Jesus Christ did not suppress, he gave his teachings or thoughts on how to live a better, kinder more compassionate life and he did, and does not want this old paradigm to cling to his teachings!

Let others breathe the fresh air of knowledge and have faith, a gentle faith all is as it should be. Love God and others enough to know this earth is not flat as was once told, and this same energy of suppression must go, before humanity can move forward. I am in this very concerned, for the knowledge of our physical heritage does not take away from our divine one, the two are intertwined, we are spirit, of God, God's creation here for a physical existence, but we need to evolve, to move on to become something greater, and that can't happen if freedom of speech and thought is suppressed.

One could say that these people genuinely believe the earth was created in six days and on the seventh God rested! Oh, I am here now at the behest of Lord Melchizedek to write of something my soul needed to say, and this flowed. I like so many other people have been suppressed, oppressed and subjected to all manner of insult in my time of service in God's light, this and other lifetimes. I have seen firsthand the damage intolerance has done, particularly suppression of the feminine, but we evolve or are meant to, we are not meant to hold onto old habits which cling. Souls come to earth not to repeat old mistakes are over and over again in the name of religious intolerance.

So why can't we just allow rational thought to flow and accept we are more. The earth is more than we were told. We are ageless when you consider we are energy, and part of a larger energy, that of God and the cosmos. Lessons aside we should perhaps have as humanity evolved passed clinging to such rigidness. Science is here to stay, and so is faith.

It is time to see that ancient texts and the bible are symbolic words written at another time in history and changed over and over again, but it has value, wisdom hidden within the words. Do you truly believe a loving God said "kill your son"?

My pain is; this has brought up in me an awareness there is so much more to do to awaken humanity, and to do it with love.

If my words are in any way sounding judgmental, I apologize. It just frustrates me that we have come so far on a journey to enlightenment, but I have faith in God, myself and you and in science, that a new theory will come about of a creation energy exceeding any so far portrayed, of a man called Jesus, who was a man, one who loved humanity enough to try to show a better way, and he opened his heart and said. "Love one another as I love you". He didn't say, "this is my own and only way", just the opposite, he loved, defied opposition and ignorance, and he loved all of the untouchables, and he so dearly honoured women, and made an attempt to show a way forward by taking women into his inner circle of initiates.

To one was he was to give his mantle after the crucifixion; to Miriam was he to leave his role, but as with all things influenced by the mass consciousness of that time, it went to Peter who opposed Miriam (Mary) and the feminine.

My point here is if a religion based somewhat on his teachings has taken root, and now oppresses and tries to slow the growth of humanity, does it really speak of a spiritual faith in God and His Son, I think not! It speaks of an established organizational thought trying to protect itself from freedom of thought, and there is pain in that, for it is not what He wanted, Jesus didn't want to start a new religion, just to show a way to live! May Light show the way.

Virginia

PAKISTAN - EASE THEIR PAIN & RESPECT FOR PRESIDENT OBAMA

What is it that keeps us from opening the heart? It is such an easy question to answer for some, they will tell you of past hurts, generations of hatred and victimisation and the nonstop opponents of their cause to find personal direction and comfort, some for economic wealth, and to others all they want is to know the deep feeling of connection to God, or their perception of God. But the subject of God is such a taboo, we are not meant to question old beliefs and doctrines handed down through the centuries. It defies logic that Love is the exclusive domain of a particular religion or culture or country.

Don't you think it's time we saw a new light in the skies, one of our own making, a pure radiant light of understanding, a new truth that we are the chosen ones. All of us from whatever culture, colour, nation or belief system, and the exclusive right to God is just an illusion, held and perpetuated by some so that there is a reason to hold power and others at bay. It can give a feeling of superiority to feel that only we are to be saved, to think that this religion or that one will be dammed and outcast, and not permitted into heaven.

Well I am told we are now at the cross roads with a big sign saying, "this way home" and by home I am speaking about a divine right to come home to God, even if one perceives God as a mighty energy, whatever the concept, God does not have a preference for only this religion or that one. In fact I am assured that religion which has served a purpose for some people in the past is now a barrier to harmonious blending of humanity, that and a judgment of only a certain country or people being chosen.

The divine right to speak for God has been given to me, for along with many others on the earth plane now, I, we see the truth as monumentally important, that all are loved equally.

How easy it would be to wait around for someone to come and lift us to the heavens to see a New Jerusalem, but only for the chosen ones. Oh that has been the past conditioning and habitual patterning for humanity. To wait for a messiah and give power to that 'one' and not recognise our own divine purpose and heritage. I realise some people would be shocked to think that I even offer the opinion that we are cosmic in origin, are made of star stuff; we are created in God's image.

Well that image we have as mankind really tarnished, and sadly don't seem to be able to break out of, that conditioned response that we are powerless and not worthy of love. I have a job to do if it is only to share love anyway I can, through energies and words.

What threat is it to put aside old beliefs, and at least open the mind enough to see the potential for God to want us home? All of us regardless if one is a Jew, or Palestinian, Catholic or an Atheist. We all evolve our way with the conditioning and lessons we have chosen before we came here. What are these lessons?

When we incarnate we are born with amnesia, and this is a protective mechanism for us to learn our self chosen lessons, and enter the earth plane and strive through various ways to remember who we are. We can do so with hard lessons and difficult circumstances, or the so called easy way. But when we come to a fork in the road where decisions need to be made we have choice and free will, but the ultimate goal is not earthly comfort, it isn't to prove how powerful, beautiful or wealthy we are. We are simply put here for one reason, we chose to learn, to recognise there is more to life that living an easy life, or one which cheats others of their power or rightful path to dignity of spirit. Our purpose is to remember who we are!

To my mind a great injustice has occurred and is still perpetuated and enhanced, to use religion as a reason to knock others down.

America was blessed with the opportunity to learn through a new way of thinking and dealing with troubles, economic and political. Where before was a leadership not of harmony, compassion and light, one which used false ideologies and descriptive judgment of others to endorse a view and war, there came a President of great wisdom and compassion. One who was of a background not known to many people, not because he was a Muslim which was gossip spread to attempt to pull him down and instill fear based thinking into a country so in need of loving compassionate leadership. No I speak of the fact he was the greatly revered Abraham Lincoln at another time in history?

It didn't take long before the knives came out, the gossips and innuendo, a scare campaign that the president was secretly a Muslim. I observed, the news and sighed, and wondered why we as mankind feel a need to dis-empower others we don't necessarily agree with. I saw a movement of fear begin to eat at a country that needs all the help they can get.

Let me ask you, as a human being, is it such a threat to allow others their beliefs? Would it truly matter if President Obama was a Muslim or a Jew, or a Hindu or a Buddhist? Do we have to feel safer by pushing others into a box so we can judge them?

Isn't it time to let the old ways drop aside and become open to freedom of thought and the distinctive ability to be pliable, flexible and see that old boxes no longer fit us. I have been asked to write in the Goddess section; to give my views to complement Lord Melchizedek's, and to bring up subjects I feel will raise issues for the whole.

How can we as the human race survive if we tear ourselves apart, constantly wanting to upstage, unseat or find a sense of self or power at someone else's expense? This is not loving and it makes me sad when I hear supposed 'Christians', many of them clergy or priests, casting judgments of other religions and enforcing this illusion only they are loved, and only the chosen ones are coming home.

The chosen ones are those innocent of heart and soul who love God with all of their heart, and that means loving all of creation, and even those who are now unaware of God. I felt heart sore to see at a time a great suffering in Pakistan, with many thousands dead, and twenty million homeless, suffering, and possibly at threat of disease and worse, that a rally was held by 'Christians' in America on the day of Martin Luther King's remembrance day. What I thought are they doing? They have no idea of the real teachings of Jesus Christ! Where is the compassionate outpouring of love to people suffering, no they need to try to pull down a president and interrupt a memory of a compassionate human being who was sacrificed to hatred.

We are at the junction now, of choosing compassionate understanding and finding a better way, or to follow the old worn out path followed for so long by those unable to let go of judgment and fear, for this is what fear is. It empowers movements of division and disharmony. To some people I being female would seem wrong to even speak these words. But humanity has no more time to wander in the darkness, and we will shift of our own accord or miss the boat so to speak, and not follow the light of understanding home. And in truth that is all we are here for. It is so simple and yet we try to make life so complicated. All life is precious!

Lord Melchizedek said to me "you playing small doesn't serve the world, it is time to take your power and be all you are, not that illusion created over time" and this applies to every one of us without exception, but it must start now with a gentle introspection of our patterning, and to see if we are one of those who are unable to think for themselves. To love God is to love all life, not some life, all life!

My heart cries out to the people of Pakistan in their time of pain. I was blessed some time ago to be invited over to stay with a holy man who was feeding the many homeless and starving. I saw the reverence shown to me and a friend in my time there, such love and gentleness and respect. I also saw more reverence for God in the people I saw living in a garbage tip than many people who call themselves 'religious' in the western world. I grieve for their pain, the people of Pakistan, and as Gods children should we not we pouring aid in, offering help and loads of food?

We are here for a self chosen lesson, how we live this life will come back to us as a reflection we may not want to see on departing this life.

Please if you value life, value God or divine creations open your heart and offer help, if you have little give what you can, never with the thought, 'what will I get back'?

This is not God's way, the Creator honours free will, and even our right to not come back to a remembrance to love, but it is such a lonely powerless road to follow.
In the name of love aid them please!
Virginia Melchizedek.

HELIOS & VESTA –
FROM THE CENTRAL SUN -
A REMEMBRANCE, WE ARE DIVINE.

We are but one part of a greater creation, Comic beings all, and yet we have lost our memory of this divine heritage. Ponder this please, we are at a point in human evolution where we can continue to just exist, procreate and merely get through each day and survive thinking only of what to buy to lift the spirits, or where to find the next round of inspiring moments to try to connect us to something greater, but what? What it is that preoccupies our lives and thoughts continuously, have you thought about this?

Where did you really come from, and where are you going, and do your actions thoughts and deeds really matter?

I have been through a period of rapid adjustment to physical needs being corrected, feeling physically challenged by negativity to think only from self interest, the self at the exclusion of the whole, a period of time where fear overcame the higher self's connection to my own divinity out of concern for survival of this body which holds my soul and aspirations of fulfilling a new consciousness for myself and others.

Some months ago Lord Melchizedek said,. "You need to get through this and come out of it aware of the real purpose for your life, to see your own power and hold this for the whole" and I didn't have a clue what he was talking about. For background information I needed to have a total bi lateral knee replacement, my soul had brought about the situation to learn from that we are far more than the physical, we are beings of infinite possibility and light, but along the way we have learned and been conditioned to see only the physical needs for pleasure, for greed, and to fill our emptiness, and perhaps the hardest of all lessons is to look at fear and feelings of unworthiness to lift ourselves out of this illusion humanity has created that of separation from God.

At this point I will add here there were ample opportunities to allow fear in, fear for survival of the body, allowing the separation to grow, but in truth I am extremely blessed to not only have had a magic surgeon, but also an opportunity to grow through facing many issues and tests.

What I did not see at all in this time of trial was unworthiness, but in fact the great blessing we are given to have free will and create our own course. Lord Melchizedek explained, "When this period of trial is over, I will not write until you do, you will lift yourself out of this illusion and grow and lift others with you" and this completely left me lost for words.

One could say it is a golden opportunity to grow through pain, but to me this wasn't the problem at all, just the negativity connected to fear which lingers in our lives if we allow it too, and a sense of separation where my guides always all loving, and definitely attentive, held back saying; the world is going to enter a painful period, where faith and hope are needed and you need to see this, we can't show it to you, or do this for you. And so it has been for the past three months processing operations and discomfort, that's the physical part but inconsequential, the really important lesson in this was not having my loving Master guides explaining every day where I would be growing and showing me the next part of the journey.

The pain was nothing really; the hard part was the feeling of separation from the divine light I feel every day of my life. What is this lesson about, I pondered. If this is so very important to the whole, what is it I am to come out of this with that will enable me to make a difference?

For some people the thought they are divine cannot possibly enter their thoughts, because the presumption we are connected to God, to Great Architect of the Universe or whatever you want to call God, is a presumption of greatness that only those with huge egos can hold. But may I tell you something, my journey has been a long and difficult one at times learning that human beings can be most cruel and selfish, and at the same time learning that these same beings have had that illusion of separation forced into their consciousness.

We have as humanity throughout the ages; through religion, superstition, and dominant aggressive thinking become subservient, we cannot see the goodness in ourselves or others, let alone see the divine in others.

It came to a time of a seeming removal of my blessed connection for me to realise that what I have to give is hope and understanding of our pathway. I will add my wonderful guides were with me constantly, healing and strengthening me, it was me who shut the feeling of divine connection off, because at times fear and discomfort came in.

Many brilliant writers throughout history have spoken about human problems, cultural deficits and behavioural aberrations which do not aid the human condition, there have been many books written to help us understand there are aspects of humanity we do not yet appreciate, and this I do see as needed, that we learn to see goodness and incorporate this and the realization we are divine.

Over the past thirty years or more I have been given prophetic visions of possible events yet to befall humanity, and I agonised over them thinking, 'why have these if I cannot change anything, cannot stop these events and trends'? I have learned we are not victims, we each choose with free will our path every step of the way, every joyful moment, and every moment of pain, and learning the hard way. We are not powerless but powerful beyond words, we are creator beings in very real terms.

We call into action circumstances, and people to learn by, and we choose when to leave the earth and when to arrive. We are resplendent beings of brilliant light, and only we can separate ourselves from God. We need no intermediary, though over time the conditioned thinking has been we are sinful and unworthy, and a representative of some religion is needed as a go between.

Oh no, we as a species have been shaped, nurtured at times, and at others blatantly and forcefully been conditioned to conform, to behave as we should like dutiful, subservient beings. But it is time to stop this illusion of separation and take our full power back now. To be responsible for our decisions and actions and negotiate a new and better way for ourselves and this planet we as humanity try to 'conquer'.

Throughout all I have been through, there is one thing which has become clearer and more powerful, my absolute awareness I am of God and hold an energy for others to also recognise their own divinity and grace. I am a child of God, but so is every being on this planet and beyond. Never has there been a better time for this expansion of consciousness as now, and with a power which flows from Helios and Vesta I do reclaim my power and rightful connection to God within, but also to release this divinity in all of creation.

To some, life is hard and unreasonable, there is an absence of love, and a time of toil and unconscious weariness without regard for the spiritual aspect or respect for the soul. We are at the point in human history where we can modify the behaviour which says think of number one first, this survival of the fittest thinking will never again be ok.

Over the last few weeks a new divine energy has been flowing from Helios and Vesta, from the sun and into our energy bodies to open up this awareness of responsibility for life, not just as a physical being, but also as a divine being here to honour all life and resurrect our way of life to see a new way forward.

We have gone through this doorway and unconditional love will permeate every cell of every being so that there is a shifting.

No longer can we be separated from God, we are the flock, and it is our time to remember who we are and return home. Some to an understanding that life is more than the day to day grind and survival of the fittest. Some will issue a statement to their soul, 'move me forward; I await this direction and am open to it'.

There is a movement coming over the next few months to remind humanity of their responsibility as divine beings to care for all life, and unfortunately many souls will go, have a transition of the body and go home. In a world gone mad with greed and decline in compassionate thinking there will be an unfortunate time to remember we are responsible for all of our actions and inactions.

The greatest blessing we can possibly have is to know who we are and where we come from, and how interconnected we are with all life everywhere, not just this planet, but on a cosmic level. We have now the opportunity to change this world, by expansion of our thinking, and unfortunately the only way some people will learn is the hard way, and that is sad, but ultimately we create and reap our own actions. Recently with the new influx of cosmic energies to aid our transformation ,karma has now turned instant. No longer is there the luxury of waiting for humanity to awaken and remember who they are and why they are here.

The cosmic cannot afford for one species to decline in growth so much they destroy all life, and this is tragic but needed. There would be many who would love to cry out, "why is God doing this to us". But beloveds you are divine and yet you do not act that way, do not treat other creations or beings with respect nor as divine, and the fall from light, the ever downward spiral of decline must halt, be stopped. There is no more time to waste.

Economic disasters - to economies should have shown us we are on the wrong track, that greed and irresponsibility is rife and getting worse. Normally decent people have begun to think that economic sovereignty over others is the only way, and such a decline has come about, but what of our connection to God?

Do you really think God wants or cares about how many cars we have, how big our houses are, or whether one attends only 'this' religion, church, or not? God has asked me through my Masters and my own soul connection to look now at ways of helping people through the times ahead.

I pondered so many times how to do so, thinking as we often do when negativity abounds to see only our physical limitations, to not let the divine self speak and hold sway. I am so very grateful that I have such a loving connection to my Creator, but equally I am so very saddened so many people now are going through such pain and trials, and many more to come, and it won't be easy, it won't be easy to listen to the higher self when climate events are reminding us of our vulnerability, or our responsibility. But in all this there is a very great blessing, one that will help all of us to be all we are, to reclaim our rightful heritage and grow.

We are not here on earth now to hoard, to create a portfolio and serve the god of greed, but to be love, to see love as there for all people, regardless of their belief systems and religions or lack thereof. God has no attachment to our physical daily events other than to love us through them, and sometimes we need to find that love for ourselves, to search it out, to say "God I am here for you show me what your will is for my life", as I once did a long time ago, at a very painful time of my life. I can tell you from experience if you call and ask, God will answer, possibly not as you imagine.

With me it was as a great windswept around the room and settled around me and left me wrapped in a love so divine I never wanted to be separated from it. Perhaps it is because I have experienced my Father's love first hand for so long I couldn't understand why when going through the past months I had no real sense of this love, and yet I knew I was loved, protected and cared for everyday. But often we do not see the lesson while we are in it; it took separation and a lot of opposition to show me what the purpose was.

Others possibly do not have that joy of feeling constantly that divine connection, the separation is complete and therein is the sadness, there cannot be a feeling of coming home when divine love seems so distant and meant only for others, for those blessed or divinely graced. But do you know we are all blessed, and we have all the help we need now, the cosmic wraps us in energy to allow this remembrance of our divine heritage. Until this very moment I did not see why I needed to experience this, now I do, to share this with you, so no matter what you or your family are going through hold onto God whatever you conceive the Creator to be, you were and are created in God's image and yet we do not act like it, nor do we feel as loving as we could.

My job is to aid you see the changes coming as not of Gods making but our own. As a collective humanity create the circumstances, we do the damage which now rebounds upon us around the world, and yet do political leaders respond with far sight, a greater vision, no an economic close down takes place, and once more the spiral of fear takes over. I am asked to remind you who you are, and prepare you for the times ahead with empowerment of your potential for greatness and love.

We can do this, recreate our world and we may need to look at the distant future as an opportunity to change all those aspects which have limited humanity over time, the greed and opportunism which is definitely not of God. Welcome as I do change, not with fear, but with an impassioned heart reaching out to those in need, sometimes it is in giving the most do we receive a glimpse of heaven on earth, the reflection of divinity shining from the face of others in need.

Blessings.
Virginia

COMPASSION

Love with all its expenditure of energy comes not from an absence of energy, but straight from God whatever we conceive this omnipotent energy to be. Love, that exasperating heady energy, which takes one's life and spins it around and leaves us breathless at times, is more than passion, though passion has a place in movement of energies. Without passion life would be a constant and unrewarding ride of ups and downs, and without those heady moments of motivation to move forward, to progress, and I am not now speaking of passion only as a motivational energy associated with sexual drive. I am speaking of passion, a deep thirst, a deeper love, and need to do something with such powerful energy.

Oh how sad the world would be without passion for life, for self-improvement and setting new career goals. Passion inspires us, but where does this flow come from if not a constant flow of love pouring into our energy bodies providing drive to do more, be more. But passion as I see it is not that which drags down, it builds up, and passion as given in spiritual terms motivates that deeper profound need to fulfill our soul journey.

Many of us are never far away from our soul destiny, that impulse which comes from deep within, a soul satisfaction when on course, and inner sadness and feeling of disconnection when detached from this life flow called God.

Many would object to the word passion and God used in the same sentence. There is such a misunderstanding of God, perhaps that is because God has been objectified, qualified into an image that is marketable.

God is, it's that simple. A power beyond belief, but God for want of a better word to describe the indescribable has such a passion for life and creation. Out of joy, supreme love and an understanding of the need for gainful employment of our life force gave us the propensity to see life from two viewpoints, one of optimism and joy and therefore a wave length which is accessible and compatible with divinity, or to create a negative vortex, an energy whereby we surrender the joy and passion to complete what we came here for.

We incarnated beings are here for a purpose to live and love and surrender that downward spiral of disconnection from the flame of life, to become, but to become what; creator beings all, but not as some have done, those energy beings who took the gift of free will given to them and explored lower energies, to draw others also into their downward spiral, but to lift, to shine and become awakened, and we have just over one year, a little more perhaps where this momentous opening of energy exists for us all to awaken and come home.

The kingdom of heaven is within, Jesus Christ said, but so did I recently as I saw a child so caught up with the heavy presentation given by formalized religion. She gave me this example of children still being bombarded with heavy dogma and closed viewpoint, I needed to explain, God, all powerful, ever loving and beautiful is within each and every one of us, and all we need to do is to be still and listen, allow our soul to speak, quiet the mind and relax and truly listen to that still small voice within, for in this space we can find God, hence "Be still and know that I AM God"

How many children around the world are still being taught that God is distant, inaccessible-that angry old man sitting in the sky ready to caste judgment. I saw that innocent child smile when I explained that God so loves us, he/she created us so that we could experience life in all its complexities and on that journey remember who we are; that the kingdom of heaven is within each and every one of us no matter what we have done on this difficult journey of discovery.

I saw this little one beam with a light so great it made me smile because I saw a light go on in her heart as she grasped the fact that God loves us so much he/she wants to experience life through our eyes- to help us discover we are not lowly creatures of sin, but divinely blessed. And at any time in our lives we can say God I am here for you. That is all that is needed; all beings of light and love must have permission to show themselves, to be invited to aid us remember, and they will be there for us anytime we ask, Arch-Angels, Angels, Ascended Masters, guides, and they have always been there for us. We just need to ask, to call out and say "guide me", but in this time of awakening no longer are we to see ourselves as given throughout historical conditioning that promoted image of sinners and of being the unworthy.

No, instead be one invited to awaken and remember, it is time to come home, but not in serious tones, and with a view that divinity and all beings of light are serious, overly pious and without humour. The fastest way home is to lift energies, laugh, and play, be as innocent children and let go of struggle- to be gentle, compassionate. Within the word compassionate, is passion- a zest for life which exists on all levels, all dimensions of God's kingdom, creations, multidimensional levels of existence; many mansions and all of them filled with passion.

Love is such a gentle energy, but it can rock our world and overnight turn it around so that only love holds sway. All it needs is for us to rejoice, let go of heavy energies and need for judgment, to see a world of compassion is the best option, for compassion upholds the two worlds, that divine kingdom, love of the divine, and this earthly existence so a natural flowing of life force can flow all can utilize on earth.

Such a pure light flows now from so many around this world and beyond who do see a new way of life as there for them now, and love as the only way home. Ask yourself, if today I encountered my higher aspect would I feel at home or would unworthiness seep in, if so then remember it is time to surrender old paradigms of thought which said, to be near God one must be humble, oh yes humility is needed, but also wisdom to know when it is time to give away that which no longer serves us, an image of us being less than divine, we are not honouring God by being less than we can be.

Take one day at a time but remember to laugh, play and find joy; to love unconditionally is the fastest way home, and it is so very easy to love.

Blessings
Virginia

ETERNAL LOVE

Life that joyful pursuit of love speaks of joyful moments, reflections and openness, and yet how often do we truly feel in love with life? Is it a common occurrence that love fills us so fully there is no doubt about the goodness of life?

I have recently seen life this way, with a few exceptions, a momentary lapse of concentration or rather openness to flowing with the life force which permeates the air we breathe. All life is perfected love when given true form, true life that is, not the illusory world many still follow, a captured form of life; contorted and strangled of joyful appreciation of the small things. Daily now life becomes more beautiful, an endless flow of love streaming from a cloud, a tree, the song of a bird, or a child's laughter, love feels the air and yet how we are taught largely to disregard this constant flow is eternal bliss.

All life is love, and nonlife two, it is the most divine of gifts to practice our free will to embrace life with love, to live each day so inspired with love and appreciation we cannot be separated from all forces of the natural world, the majesty of mountains or the wild moving of a savage sea. I see love in all life, but in the human family a sadness prevails, a longing for something lost, not yet seen, and a thirst comes to drink of knowledge of something greater, and all along it is within our reach. A simple word love, such a simple yet powerful word to entice a most ardent heart to crave something more, but may I tell you how I perceive this love to be, a movement of some potential force unknown to us so there is fear. We often fear to open up to love in case it hurts, or once felt that it fades away or is trodden beneath the hardships of life, but this is the difference between a world of eternal love and the present world the way the majority of the population see it. Love is not for them because they are deemed unworthy, or worst sinners.

We are all I feel capable of total love and blending into this new world being created as I speak. A nourished view of love flows to us all now constantly, issues from God constantly, ever loving, fully nurturing the beloved. Love streams forth as a constant flow, eternally without favour, open to all equally. God loves us all so deeply, I feel it every day this divine love, and I am no different to anyone else, just a soul upon the path of discovery, and you know the greatest discovery I have made. It isn't in daily searching through superfluous actions, shopping trips, or the daily grind, but in having the trust of a child to be open to life forms flowing to us constantly being emitted there every moment of every day.

I have my moments where conditioned reflexes kick in once more, and societal conditioning says be aware, have fear, don't allow vulnerability, others will hurt you – the fear factor permeates our thinking. It has been a very valuable tool used over the ages for crowd control, to use to bludgeon or bully those awakening to conform, to respond as all others do, but without love being the prime motivating factor.

Love is the one energy which is free from fear, and it is so very beautiful! I have seen the fear in many people's eyes, those coming for a healing, and this fear cripples bodies and closes down energies for growth, true purpose is right there for us all to reveal.

Energies are now being beamed to us for planetary enlightenment to allow us to awaken, but to what? What is it that is so important the cosmic lovingly flows this energy to enrich our lives, but also to awaken us to the fact we are star stuff! We are made of something greater, a luminosity of such profound beauty is really our true form. We have but to open our hearts and feel the eternal connection, it is there in every flower, bird, fish, mountain, and in every creature from the largest to the smallest molecule.

We are the contradiction, our intellect and ego places us at the centre of our universe, but we are foreign to it because we allow the ego and fear to generate more of the same. I love my life with all of difficulties and challenges for they make me stronger, I love every minute of it because even in the conflict, in shedding onion skins so to speak there is growth, and with each illusion of separateness gone we become more radiant and pure, but there is no superiority in becoming, all life strives to become one. For some forms of life there is a natural flowing, and necessary habits to survive, we have the advantage, and remembering who we are at our fingertips.

God and all of the divine helpers aid us at every turn to become more aware, and so it is now a new energy prepares to flow, opening us to a new a higher frequency -vibration, one activated by love.

It is an expanding universe, and it opens us now to the enormity of our being, for in reality we are endless, limitless, and we are of God, therein is the word love, known to me as a gift I will Cherish, I hope you do to.

Blessings.
Virginia

WE ARE MADE OF SOMETHING GREATER, WE ARE STAR STUFF.

A nourished view of life comes only when given power from within, that gossamer thread of comprehension one has that direct line to God is but a moment away when held onto. Faith brings with it a spoken word of love, love as given forward direction through loving remembrance of one's path.

How is it that one life cascades into another and is lost to memory upon this pathway of remembrance, the given form fades away to reveal pure spirit once more. An earthly life is but transitory, momentary, and guarded with so many lost memories, lost to the passages of time. Life goes on but without memory, soft and tender of that journey of soul all make to remember in total a fused passageway of love.

Love, gentle reminder of our true heritage is there as gestures and moves one makes to show devotion for others, but yet the truly beautiful source of love is hidden from view, a veil has come down to record only that existence lived, one metamorphic moment of time called life.

How is it that at times the most exquisite of all loves is hidden from view, if not by the extraordinary effort placed into carving a new life, one cut off from divine love. It does not serve to go into the pain achieved in this separation; it does not aid the journey to speak only of the trials of life.

Let me speak of love as I know it, a priceless love of service of the common good, but also a journey of ecstatic experiences, graces shown and felt, and through the veil of non remembrance comes a moment of connection, but to what?

What is it that in body we do not so easily feel now? A connection deep and soothing in its love, and sympathetic in its memory coded messages, that we are loved by a force unseen, but felt deeply at times. A love as no other!

We are star stuff; we come not from an earthly realm, but one of non space, nonmaterial formation. We are eternal and graced with the beauty unimaginable, and yet in this earthly form all connection to divine love and grace is hidden from view. We are just beginning to see, to feel beyond a veil of illusion, that which separates and convinces us all this earthly existence is all there is.

No man has yet found that direct route back home, save one, and he was given form only for a limited time to teach the way of love - love as does come from God, Creator, and lover of all beings. Such is the pathway given form now that one can awaken daily. Momentary periods are available now for us to see beyond the veil, to see beyond and love life enough to become. But if we are born into this existence without memory of past lives, or others, how can we verify this is true, when we have been taught that we are but sinners with one life to lead and then we die and are no more?

Do you remember that story given as teachings of old, that religions hold all power and connection to God, I do! It has been drummed into the consciousness of mankind for so long now many millions see only this, not the continuous lifetimes which follow where the soul goes on and decides what lessons there are still to learn. We have been here before, and we will again. The circle of life goes on, and one must judge ourselves at the end of life and determine what if any aspects of life need to change! How much better we could have loved and lived with compassion, and how we could help others remember our divine heritage, our pure connection to God.

Is it possible that there will be a day religions let go of control of power wrongly used to mislead the masses into thinking they have no direct line to God?

Life is so much more than we presently see or feel. A momentary glance catches at times something so wonderful, so beautiful in its energy, the breath catches, and in that moment of recognition we do see and feel we are one with all of creation, God. In that moment joy is felt, and then a smile comes, a hint of remembrance that we are more, we are star stuff!

We are not lonely creatures who need to fight and squabble and hit out or take others power.

We are more than we presently show the world now, and many people upon reading this will remember a frozen moment in time when they truly glimpsed that remarkable moment of connection to the Creator and to creation, and the deep peace and profound beauty which comes like a thief in the night, this energy silently moving around us raising our consciousness with love to awaken, just this; not a moment of remembrance frozen in time, but to awaken us fully to the divine beings we truly are! So we can let go of this illusion we are living in separation.

How much more beautiful will our lives be when we all see and feel this divine connection and live it daily as perfected beings, just as Jesus Christ did, and we have only to allow the energy now being beamed to us now to permeate our beings and let go of false beliefs, that we are not capable of connection to God.

Love is all we were created from, it is our natural form without the dross of false teachings. Life in all its ecstatic beauty awaits us now daily; the Sacred Feminine enters our beings to bring balance back to a war weary world. The Sacred Feminine flows now gently, softly, to alight upon your brow and bless you with a love of unconceivable beauty, one which nourishes and soothes and calms the soul, to give the memory of your Source.

We enter now a time in human history not seen before, when enlightenment energies beam out, and yes sadly backward movement will come from those stuck in fundamentalist energies, thoughts of constriction, anger and judgment and scrutiny of others. Such a sad movement comes now across the world. In many places instead of evolving and fitting this new energy by opening the heart, darkness, fear, drives these sad people to close down and start to persecute others who are open and flowing.

Such male dominated aggressive energy moves around the planet now, centers of male domination, the feminine suppressed and only a glimmer of freedom seen from this dominant energy, but this feminine energy now flows to all of creation, to soothe, and to be the gentle healing balm all need to transcend beyond the worldly events which pull down energies.

Love that healer of creation flows now as does the gentle energy of God- Creator flow now the feminine energy, that passive regenerative comforting energy to all of creation.

Love flows now, respect this loving energy, and allow it to heal all of creation, to softly, gently restore memories of the Creator and our own divinity.

In Eternal Light I Bless You.
Virginia

PEACE TALKS

God so loved, he/she created, but what was it that was created, and for what reason? What possible reason could there be for God to wish into reality a creation in which energies conflicted? How can this decision be understood?

My recollections of life as it was meant to be came to me clearly upon a moment of realisation there was and is one deliberate plan in place, but what value is there to create a species so conflicted that violence and hatred are shown daily, if not by example of surrender of lower aspects gained by fruitful reflection, a slow realisation over time that this species of which we are a part are made in God's image, but for what purpose?

What a gift of love we have to be seen worthy of being set free to embrace free will and exemplify the greater aspects of love. Along the creative pathway of surrendering came of our own awakened state of consciousness, a moment given by our souls a separation from God seen as needed and in this state to embrace the higher aspects which reflect the grace of God flowing through us.

When given free will, we slumbering creations chose to see from a closed viewpoint; to give our power away and allow others to set the rules and parameters for personal and spiritual growth, and in such an unawakened state we were given guidance from those higher beings, who out of love chose to ease our pain and lead us gently back into the reality of love, and what a job they have had. Whether called angels, masters, guides, divas, those light beings of divine grace and love have implemented God's plan every step of the way. At certain points of time the historical message was encoded, given messages came to awaken us from our slumber, the ignorance of separation from creation.

All along the feminine aspect of God dismissed, overlooked, and eroded the vision of God as a complete energy frequency with both masculine and feminine energies. What was a creation of balance became unbalanced, and into the slumber came a preponderance of masculine energies, a patriarchal system evolving out of ignorance, and fear of the feminine as tempter of man.

Oh how God saw this and was saddened, for the feminine aspect is love, and after all isn't God love? Love flows freely from God, divine aspect of life, lover of creation, lover of beauty. Devotion to creation came from both balanced male and feminine energies, and in this rich environment, that of divine lover, creation came about. All love is but energy flowing freely into all realms of being, all layers, dimensions and opportunities for growth. When love is absent fear predominates, and so humanity has evolved through cycles of slumber, all of them aided from on high, to awaken us before we miss one opportunity of such profound joy.

So it is we as an awakening species are choosing, empowered by free will to create the divine here on earth. Some sadly still do cling to the illusory world of fear, of separation, and masculine dominated energies, and in this state we now evolve to a point of reaching a pinnacle of growth where all flow into a dimensional doorway, open to all upon reconnection with the divine flame.

Love, that awakened state of joy, of perfected vision where all of creation is valued and seen as sacred, this vision of my world I see now as a natural outpouring of my father/mother and yours, but in this illusionary view of world peace I see it quite differently to Lord Melchizedek.

I bring to this discussion of world peace one public sorely missed in discussions held to open the Middle East to new flows of understanding, and I state this is my view not of an appointed view by Lord Melchizedek.

I a created empowered feminine being of light have been to the Middle East, sent there by the Hierarchy to awaken energies in others, in me, and gain an understanding of the complexity of the region. I have seen the hostility there on both sides, and I will now clearly state that both sides have an aggressive attitude to the feminine, be it subconscious and defensively conscious in outwardly aggressive and defensive energies.

Do you know what the world needs in simple terms, a return to love, to balance, and see through the eyes of God, a lover of eternity and beauty. God, creator of perfection and design, created all with one thing in mind, that he/she could experience life through all of creation, a perfectly balanced creation in the beginning. One which has been eroded by us as a species, with free will we have in our unawakened state allowed the balance to be lost, and so love was lost, it's that simple.

I have been in Israel and seen in some heavily religious areas the aggressively superior attitude to women, to femininity, and that superiority flows out in aggressive moves to hold onto power.

At the moment Israel is not a balanced nation in my view. Love is missing! Oh yes there are our institutionalised churches and places of worship, all aggressively defended so much so no divinity resides there, and in Palestine also I have seen the aggressive masculinity taking over. No sides in this conflict are without some merit, but both have lost softness. There cannot be healing of a world out of balance, and where religious ideologies and laws and doctrines aggressively dismiss the feminine.

In doing so it is saying God's perfect design was flawed, and that is strongly felt now in a clash of religions and cultures preparing to lash out at each other, both seeing superiority and using historical concepts which were only ever guidelines wrongly interpreted, and changed progressively to write out the importance of the feminine.

What the world needs now is love, a world as God created it, a perfected view of joy in both male and female working together, in a graceful recognition of each other's attributes.

Love is the most powerful energy in creation, and yet it is rendered impotent, weak and unresponsive when balance is not present.

I saw the sadness in the eyes of both Palestinians and Jewish people who don't want to continue to exist in a world of hatred and violence, but the air is so thick with fear and hatred in this area, that love has an uphill battle to sustain light in the very place which now claims to be the centre of light for the promised people. But do you know, all love, all hope it isn't lost, because we stand at the doorway of opportunity to open that last gateway and allow in the divine, but the concept is entirely different to that one told of old, for this gateway opens for the flocks to return home, but it isn't just for one nation or race to flow through. This gateway is for the I AM presence to enter into our consciousness, and it's a two way street. God flows to us every bit as we flow into this divine energy, the balance must come about so that the divine vision can become a reality.

We live in interesting times, (an old Chinese proverb), but how interesting it is up to us, to awaken, to love as it is, and that isn't a male dominated society to dictate the state of the world, it isn't for females to be denied education or equal status, or to view femininity as a threat to a delicate male ego. No, divinity is blessed with a sacred love of femininity every bit as much as that of masculine energies, and it is the answer to perfected love flowing a graceful year approaches, and this last opportunity enter into this doorway of awakening comes.

Can we do you think conceive of a world of equality and create it? I think we can and work to create this perfect vision of a world of peace for a thousand years. I have been shown the choices we have, and our own obstructionist ways of hindering the peace process.

Love is the way and the light, and it flows to us all now in perfected glory. We are but to open up our hearts and accept this divine opportunity, to remember who we are and come home.

In perfect love and peace I bless you.
Virginia

"KNOW THYSELF"- "KNOW THAT YE ARE GOD'S- "THE KINGDOM OF GOD IN WITHIN"

Anointing ones soul with duplicity of purpose comes to some as the most profound of problems. Awakening becomes mans sole purpose, but what of self realisation, a surrendering of forces used over time to speed our separation from God?

Oh how easy it would be to stay blindfolded, to exhaust that downward spiral of disbelief in our own divinity. How easy it would be to say,' this is my lot, why aim at the stars, I am born to a world of pain and disillusion.' It would be so very easy for us to continue this path of separation from God, to shine only dimly, and give all power away, but you know our Creator awaits us with such joy and anticipation.

It would come as no surprise to some people that pressures are exerted at times; an opposing force comes, to distract our homeward journey.

Lower energies cease to have and hold power if enough love flows. Let us break this cycle and explore that divine light in which awakened souls see a new heaven and a new earth.

Such is that impassioned plea from our own souls, think for yourselves, awaken to the gifts you have been given! Surrender that lowly aspect as portrayed over time of mankind as sinful and speak with a new language, that of compassion and hope yes, but as fully empowered beings open the heart, in this perfected energy of God's love the soul sings to delights never seen in darkness.

Oh chosen souls, my soul speaks to yours of accomplishment, of strength of purpose, and gifted ways of expelling lower energies, not with fight, with struggle, but simply to not see them anymore. Not to ignore, just to rise above lower aspects and energies, and if challenged with a face to face confrontation with darkness say, "You cease to exist!"

For in this world, we creator beings have allowed illusion to take over. We have collectively given away our divine gift in favour of that of presumed image of sinner, of being unworthy, and hence the separation began, and until this day still permeates humanities thinking.

We are challenged daily to forget the divine, the beautiful, and instead put our eyes down and stumble through life not able to see, truly see the potential for wonder and beauty. That fragile beauty of a flower is but an extension of us, for in our divine state we are part of all life, all of us without exception glow with a light within.

This misconception we are unworthy must go! It does not serve the human race any longer to serve two Gods, the one of grace, or the god of defiance that lowly energy which refuses to recognise the power of God and in time the God within. It is time to choose the God of love.

We have come so far and yet we have a little way to go in reality, just a moment to think, "The kingdom of God is within", truly means what it says. We are co creators, and in a moment of recognition we can multi task and start to change paradigms of thought, activities, and moral issues. All life can be transformed in an instants recognition. "Know Thyself" is a saying not fully under stood by the masses. To know oneself is to know God and in that moment of loving reflection take power for our lives. We are so very blessed, every day it just needs a transformation of thinking and consciousness.

'Words, some may say, words, how does this help me, I have no money, or am homeless, or my wife left me, or I have lost a loved one'. Stop and think- life is a gift we chose to experience here on earth, but why did we, divine beings all, choose to incarnate into dense energy, into body, or to experiences or circumstances which are hardly divine? Because our souls chose to take a form to experience life and remember and help others remember their source.

We are not powerless beings thrown into situations by a cruel God. We chose as empowered beings to come to earth, to incarnate and experience what can only be described as a separation, to draw others up and to remember who we are, and in those life circumstances; some of great riches, and some of poverty, learn the best lessons for our souls to grow in light, and as a whole bring about an awakening of momentous proportions.

Everyone on earth now is here to help prepare for the way for this great transformation of consciousness, not only to recreate ourselves and to let go of fear and lower energies, but to transform the world into the new kingdom of God, and we have the opportunity now.

A new dawn awaits us, one of our own making as empowered co creators. We can complain about life we came into, or change our perception, our way of thinking, and on mass instantaneously transform this world into one of joy and hope. How do I know this, because I have seen what we are and why we have come here. Every one of us is truly blessed, everyone on earth now has come to be part of this grand awakening, this time of joy and light and no one is exempt from this gift of light penetrating the very core of our beings.

We gather to us the people and circumstances we need to aid us learn, some to act as challenges to our path and some to aid us, and both should be equally blessed by us for the lessons we must learn which is our preparation for the trip home. The awakening of the flock is literally God awaiting his flock's home. We have wandered too far for too long and planetary expansion now shifts into a new gear through which wavelengths of light not yet seen or felt before come en mass with intent to aid us grow, to intuit and fill our minds and hearts with a need.

There comes now in many people a homesickness so to speak, where life as we know it just isn't enough. We are tired of wars and hatred. We are fed up with the constant bickering and pulling others down so we may feel more power, and there is now a mass awakening on the horizon of millions, billions of people seeing with new eyes and of truly being born again, not into a new religion, just to a remembrance of light and love; God's love as it permeates every atom, every cell and mind, and some will deny God for the need to aid the egos cries for power to hold sway and darkness ever the tempter of hearts tries so hard to hold onto power, but it is all an illusion- a world of our creation, from the fall from light a long time ago.

Wisdom is in knowing that light within effortlessly flows to us all without favour. God's love belongs to all equally, and with such effortless joy is heals, and our world transforms, light is everywhere, and suddenly even the most terrible circumstances dissolve before it, for there is nothing more powerful than love.

It is of concern to God that this time comes and there is a new kingdom offered, and so many are still caught up in the illusion of materialism and greed as the only god, but as we have seen economic circumstances change, why? to reflect to us the misuse of power and greed. A momentous time approaches of love filtering our systems so we no longer want to hold onto old ways.

We have free will and our light shines as a collective beacon to all those who are awakening, that we may en mass find the way home. It is such a beautiful road to follow, the way of light. Never before have we had such an opportunity to grasp a new concept so easily. Energies are being released to ease our way and allow new concepts of thought to flow. Divinity is within, and in that is truth! "Know thyself" is an ancient wisdom which only now is beginning to be widely under stood. "Know that ye are Gods", not with ego driven desire to be seen as more than others, just a perfected vision you are brothers and sisters with me, with all beings, and in that is truth.

A perfected vision of love as does flow from the sacred heart of God flows now into your consciousness, as mine, but also into the hearts and minds of all creation. Love is that energy of compassion, comfort and passion for life we can all feel now by opening the heart and mind and just feeling God; being open to the experience, but it doesn't take a building to connect. It doesn't take an intermediary, "Know ye are Gods"! speaks to the heart of all beings, of gentle love and comfort. It speaks of that loving approach being shown to others in daily life, and it speaks volumes of wisdom, all those wise words over time issued to humanity in ways to allow it to permeate our thinking.

When love enters, all darkness disappears. Love heals and transforms, it may not instantly change the situation we are experiencing, but it softens the edges and energies so change can come. To struggle, to hold on tenaciously to things, events or people is denying ones pathway which is to honour all life in every aspect of daily life, and to gently coerce obstructions out of the way. It has long been known to fight, to oppose, creates more of the same, a way to remove obstacles in our lives is to love them to death, to love them enough only energies of love surround the situation so any darkness or obstruction dissolves and is removed, and as we come to this time of quantum awakening do not think that opposition won't come, all darkness will simply give way to light. There is always the possibility for darkness to hold on tenaciously to humanity, to obstruct such a homeward journey, but in truth there is no power greater than love, for in love is God.

At such a time as the reclamation of souls, it is to be expected that greed and powers, forces for darkness would hit out at light. To think otherwise would be foolish, but cease to give it power, and as with any corrupted energy it will disintegrate and self destruct, we have need to do nothing, just love! I have seen obstruction more than many on my journey, and have been shown the power of love and light to dissolve and transmute, and on this journey I have encountered people who could not let go of ego driven need to pull down to obstruct, and I bless all of them for their contribution to the unfolding of my awareness we are Gods, co creators, but as with any power comes responsibility to do no wrong, to misuse power, and to be ever loving to ourselves and others who have difficulty with life, for when there is an absence of love fear enters.

We who now begin to awaken to our power as co-creators understand that such power as is love is never to be misused, and always given freely. What we cannot afford to do is withhold love and light out of pain of others disconnection, for there in is our separation from light. Love, that most divine energy holds us safe! Love is a gift, treasure it, but not as with a treasured gift of wealth, do not hoard this gift as it is meant for all.

Planetary awakening comes swiftly now upon the wings of love, silently and gracefully.

May love hold you in its divine care.
Virginia

THE PRICE OF LOVE

The ultimate course of love is to enhance the other, too give of one's best and enrich the lives of all those we come into contact with. To be open to love is to give a free expression of gracious acceptance of all others, but love is not weak, love is strong in content of forgiveness, but it can stand in the face of obstruction and if strong enough stand before the heaviest of judgments made by those of limited thought processes.

Such was a situation which became a tragedy, a sad reflection of the limited cultural restrictions enacted when social or cultural norms are broken. But where is love in such closed acts such as the stoning to death of a man and woman who broke strict cultural taboos created as an automatic response to control women, but also seen by some men as a very vigorous way of reinforcing laws established by men to keep a society in check?

Acceptance of situations at times is difficult, and yet do know there is a time coming not too far away when we have the potential to cut out lower energies which dominate thinking of the majority of people. Love is that energy all aspire to, and yet because of closed thinking so many shut the heart and mind to the very energy needed to reform this planet at a most crucial time.

My mind is drawn to the images on a news report of two lovers who ran away to be together, and a love that held firm even in the oppressive energies brought about to deny that shared love.

"Oh wretched mortals I have heard Leonardo da Vinci say, open your minds, cast out that deception which captures with fear and the need to suppress and persecute others for being different or thinking differently".

Love comes so seldom to those in human form. Many go through their entire lives never truly knowing love, genuine love of another human being, and the vision seen yesterday, that of two lovers stoned to death brought me to tears. Yes for the pain suffered by these two people who when faced with death by one of the most primitive modes of delivery of punishment still did not deny their love. Am I a hopeless romantic? No I don't think so, I feel for the pain of these two lovers, but even more so that there exists today beliefs so aggressively masculine and destructive.

Love that most generous of energy's was broken upon the hardened desires of those so afraid of love that no human freedom of thought can be allowed. It is inconceivable to me that in this day and age that such barbaric ideas abound, to deny others free will choice to follow a course of love. I am not privileged with information about their intent or obligations, only genuine love and concern that such love was crushed literally, stoning the form of punishment for having loved outside the rules.

We are entering a time of profound joy and love, and yet I see around me in this world evidence strongly so that negativity still dwells deeply embedded within the belief systems of many masculine dominated cultures. To my mind there is no justification for such hardened attitudes, those which punish love by insult to the body, the image of a woman cowering before a mass of men intent upon her death while crying out they defend God tears at my heart and soul, for it is so far from where we are going as humanity. But I am also very mindful of Lord Melchizedek's words which spoke of fear dominated, masculine driven beliefs breaking out to suppress humanity and make the famine and cower before their might.

Oh the sight of a woman being stoned to death in this age shocked me, and I would imagine many millions of people who do respect others' rights to think differently. Such moves to crush free will in the name of God are wrong. God did not create man and woman to be seen as cattle to be broken and punished for speaking out, or for simply wanting to love.

The hatred in the eyes of some of these men was total, so much so that there was a driven madness there, and under the guise of a religion which is meant to be compassionate and loving; the original concept was only ever of respect and compassion to be shown, not to be used as a vehicle for misogynistic women hate.

Oh this was indeed a tragic sight, and it is a warning to us all too ever be alert to being oppressed by fear, and it is there in the background that oppressive regime of fundamentalism overshadowing humanity at a time of enlightened growth.

We can look at such tragic scenes and say "oh its awful, but it happened over there" or we can say "the potential to wrongly use power is there for all of us", and to be ever alert to the fact that we have the potential to be light or darkness, and we must choose and hold the light high and secure so that no darkness can put it out.

My love poured out to this tragic man and woman, they are a reminder to us that we are on a journey with two courses, to return home to love, or to allow fear to breed and spread it poison out to corrupt and pull down energies.

We can change the world, we can, and we can shift the emphasis away from masculine dominated energies to create a more balance world, but it won't be easy, but we can do it simply by loving more, softening our attitudes and holding the light there to open the hearts of those so closed, but we can do this together, create a world of universal harmony and cooperation.

Blessings
Virginia

HEAVEN ON EARTH

I have often wondered why I have been asked to aid Lord Melchizedek, what I could add to the human consciousness that others couldn't. But it just occurred to me I am representative of the whole; one feminine aspect of humanity, one very typical example of human potential mixed with human ignorance and a lack of spiritual insight at times into our real purpose. My difficulty has always been 'why am I asked to do this, is there anything I can contribute that others perhaps could not'? The answer has always come from back from my ego no, in fact perhaps the generalization of one member of humanity holding a focus of energy is exactly why I am chosen, or self chosen.

Perhaps it is the very nature of my being, unlike many others I am simply in love with life, with Mother Earth and God, and I feel that is my qualification. Oh I know others love, but perhaps the gentle nature of the feminine comes through out of such an honouring I have for life, all life.

Not one aspect of life to me is less important than any other. I realize we are one! I feel it in my very cells and bones, my body is an example of the life force which flows through all of creation, and very much like 'Luke' in the "Star Wars" movie, I feel the force and therefore honour life, with all its eccentricities and complexities and complications, and like all others I feel the ground beneath my feet, but see and feel it as a constant reminder of our roots. Our connection to the earth is a connection to Creation and Creator.

Love flows from me, into me constantly as an extension of God, but equally I am now a being of earth, and at times disconnected from her, and in that is a statement relating to all of humanity. We are divine, we are co-creators of life, and yet so grounded not in the nurturing energies of love which flow freely from Mother Earth to nurture us, but also remind us of our very mortality on this earth. We have a very limited number of years to seal our soul destiny, to fulfill a very important task, but what is so important for us to experience on earth at this time?

Perhaps it is to see and feel our connection to the earth, to breathe in her love and nurturing and to be restored, but also by our actions and intentions honour the earth and aid her in her evolution. We are beings of clay so to speak, but our true nature is in the stars. We have come so far as humanity and yet the fundamental meaning of our very existence escapes us now, we are generally so concerned with attitudes and behaviors which keep us alienated from the earth.

When was the last time we really sat with our feet on the earth and took in her healing energies, rays of balance and restoration? When was the last time we camped by a stream and sang a song of praise for creation? How long has it been since we took a look at humanity and our disconnection from the earth, and saw the part we play in the intricate web of life? Humanity can saw with the angels, and cruise skies in jets, and yet how often do we just plant our feet on the ground and say, "yes I need balance, I am a being of light and so and divine, but I am also of this existence on earth and so imbedded in the energies of the earth, not foreign to it."

The gift I have to give that I am sure you do too is love. But how easy it is to shut off the heart and to say to God and to creation, "I am distant to you, I live in this world, one of structure and mechanisms to move us, cars, trains, boats and planes, but the simplicity and this structure of the earth is what I am truly made of". We as humanity distance ourselves from the earth and strive so hard to tame the elements, to conquer nature. How about loving her instead? When was the last time you just held a precious moment of love and respect for Mother Earth, Gaia?

I feel so very sorry for those people so shut off from life they do not see the miracle of creation every day in every moment, were a precious glimpse of sunlight upon a leaf glistens in the moisture of a drop of water and makes one gasp for the beauty of it. We are creation, it is in us, to me we are microcosms of the whole- a macrocosm of life so rich and variant in its form we should be rejoicing in creation, enhancing and honouring it daily.

Perhaps the gift I can give is love, a simple gentle love of creation, and I wish that all beings could see God's creation as I do, not as alien and harsh and something to conquer, or to get through each day without joy, just simply love, and learn to keep our feet planted firmly on the earth while realizing with the totality of our being we are one with the Creator and His creation. Therein is peace, in knowledge we truly serving a purpose on earth.

The door to divinity swings two ways, as divine light pours out love to us; we are also open to returning through this doorway too. We are divine, we have just forgotten our true heritage, so trapped are we at times with consumption of resources and life in general; the impact of life in the fast lane takes its toll, but it is in these coming years, the next year and half in particular we can enter the doorway of divinity, to not only catch a glimpse of our true nature, but also purpose.

We can then participate freely in lifting the world into a new consciousness field of discovery, we have that right, and we are given a gift of loving energies to awaken us, but also show the way home, and do you know, the easiest way I have found in touching the face of God, is to love creation and therein is the doorway. To simply touch upon and leaf, a flower, a sunset, or the flight of a bird, or the might of a wave, there is a gift, a moment of transition from one thought form or frequency to another, and it is that easy. All one has to do is love and keep love flowing and we are there, and the kingdom of God is within, but it is also in realizing that we are one with all of creation and that there is no separation if love flows.

This is the gift of knowledge given at another time in history by many wise souls to enlighten.

In Peace Profound

Virginia

PLANETARY ALIGNMENT- CARPE DIEM- SEIZE THE DAY.

Fear of any kind clouds the human condition, fear holds back energy and growth and trips humanity into increasingly decreasing spirals of form, and in this a rapid testing of one's 'metal'. The soul pushes the human being to new extremes to find the true source of power and light, the power of divine connection. A separation comes once this stage is reached, where the noble aspects begin to take hold and govern human actions.

Today marks the day a new energy streams forth into creation, a new energy of heightened expectations, of fear being dropped from the governing of policy and individual human lives.

We live a world of extremes, of the most joyful and noble of behaviors, and the lowest, that governed by fear.

When any country, group, or people functions upon fear, when politicians cater not to the highest of intentions, a descending energy then breaks down society. At that moment fear enters the thoughts and minds of people. Fear of loss of a job, or decreasing money, and fear of outsiders, hence the fear of refugees. Then can come the ostracizing people who in any way may threaten the status quo; and that includes thought patterns of individuals. Fear murders growth, and holds us as humanity into a pathetic condition where we are unable to recognize the divinity within or see other people's potentials to change.

Fear must go, and today a great alignment came about where in the days ahead a momentary fleeting burst of light goes out, like a wave across the cosmos, and this will begin to bind lower energies and inhibit fear. So much growth has taken place for humanity, and as a whole we are evolving and coming to a point where we can begin to see from a high viewpoint, but for fear as the instrument of darkness, or rather a shadow that is cast upon all of creation.

We are granted this burst of light and love as a final signal to all of creation that love heals all, seals us in gentle energies, but love will not ever bow down to fear. Today an alignment took place where there is a momentary opportunity to burst forth past fear and have it peel back its grip on humanity, but it won't be easy.

We all experience some form of fear. We try not to, we seek higher ideals and vibrations, but we do not always take up opportunities to look at fear head on. We are afraid of looking at something which causes pain and hence bury all attempts to shift, but now we are given a golden opportunity to bind fear and hold it in place, it won't be easy.

There will be many challenges to our fear of vulnerability; many hard conditions and planetary alignment has been a tool so to speak in the development of a new energy, one where we are encouraged to push harder at creating a loving society, of being tolerant, and hopefully this will give political leaders and tyrants, a reminder that fear cannot be used to hold humanity back, and also gracing leaders the courage to look at previous thought patterns, such as trying to stay in power by lowering the bar so to speak, to hold humanity back, and holding an energy at the lowest common denominator, that of public fears.

I see this day as an opportunity to step up quickly now, and seize the day 'Carpe Diem' and move forward with love as the powerful energy to shape this new world we are creating. Love will be here for us in abundance, but over the next weeks, we will all have this opportunity to shed, to cleanse, and so will the planet.

How we use this opportunity is very much up to each one of us. It is an opportunity to look into the face of God from a higher viewpoint, and to say to our fellow beings. "We are one! Let us help you in your time of trial".

I wish it to be so.
Virginia

DEFEND GOD'S LIGHT

Expectations of life can at times be so filled with doubt and fear. We often stop our growth and surrender all the light held within, but also there is an element of doubt I feel we as humanity experience daily, not just fear of where our food and shelter comes from, but how we can truly know why we are here on earth now at this great and most momentous of times. How can we really know that God is real, and how do we fit into the picture it all, are we part of creation, or just an accident which happened, and which is now described by theologians and religions as sinners on earth, but governed by God an overseeing body of power enough to create universes and the cosmos itself, and yet not able to reveal Himself to us?

Here is the quandary, we are on a planet with billions of people, the majority who believe in a God of some sort, - a God of a vengeful nature, and some who feel God is all loving but stays distant, and who doesn't really care what happens to us on our journey.

Can I explain to you now how I know my Creator to be, and I am not some religious zealot, in fact I would not consider myself to be 'religious' at all. I feel religion now is a major stumbling block to planetary healing of old wounds between people, and with care of the planet. God has always been part of me. I have known this since I was a small child, my God is a God of love and compassion - part of creation, open to all we are and experience!

God, Creator Being of love and life has touched my heart and soul with such a total acceptance of all I am, and a realization came through me God experiences Himself (for lack of ability to find a term which suits an energy of sublime love). My God cares for us, but does not judge us if we fall down and make mistakes, we are loved anyway, and opens energy daily for me to feel alive, to feel beauty in every moment of life, and to be part of Himself. I am God even as you are, and that has always been the case! God, YHWH, Creator of life gave us the ultimate gift, free will to experience, to find out how the path of life could be traveled alone, or with an intimate connection through love flowing, and in that is the greatest gift we could be given, to melt into this Being at any time of day or night, without need for a building, or a person to intercede.

God is. But what is God? God is all loving, a life force and energy, a force so great all of creation is nurtured constantly, empowered and showered with life, a life force known to some as nous, (divine order of creation) to some He is capable of giving pain and hardship and a heavy burden, punishment for our deviations upon our journey of discovery; such a hard God, one who supposedly rewards vile acts with rewards, such as giving a number of virgins in heaven, and to some God is but a point of light. But do you know something, along this journey of discovery of humanity a split came, even before humanity came into existence, into being. Energies created by God and given love and free will, some found that God's power was what they wanted, and so a divide came about, a separation, higher level beings fought for dominance and broke away from love, having been granted power of creation, and the course was set to take a rebellious stand and separate from the all embracing love of God and an attempt made to usurp God's power and grace.

Over time the ultimate gift of love was taken and twisted until a spiritual rebellion came about, which then with time flowed out to all of creation, and with the evolution of human beings the loving energies given form then began to be tempted, to gain power by use of fear and a heavy handed energy of constriction. For fear is the ultimate power to take from God His creation, and that energy is now so dominant in all sectors of the world, from world politics, dictators now fighting for their lives to keep power wrongfully gained, and through people and just like us who don't feel able to reach out and touch others, and except their beliefs and love them anyway.

I have experienced such times of fear, where opposition came, a darkened energy to cancel out the light, and we are all without exception here now awakening, or given the power to awaken. Lord Melchizedek as Universal Logos - Eternal Lord of Light has been battling to enlighten all of creation to this realization; we are part of the problem, as we are also the solution to worldly woes. We are the epitome of power and love, if our light can be developed and maintained now. Every one of us has a choice now - light or darkness, and this is not the wild imagining of a misguided woman, it is truth, and deep in your heart and soul you will feel this truth awakening within you now!

Energies are pouring down upon us to awaken us, but also to hasten our return home, and what do I mean by that? We are asked to remember our source, and our connection to that Eternal Light of Love, and honour our light and aid in the reestablishment of lights centre's the world over.

Now we are within a very narrow window of opportunity to come home, Gods flock, and turn our back on darkness which keeps humanity trapped into fear and generation of energies aided now by the antichrist to lure God's children away. In many ways is this developed- by dazzling, all sorts of distractions there to lure out of greed, and to invite by fear and by far it is the prime motivating force for all wars and division within humanity. Religion is also being used now as a tool to corrupt through fear and a sense of superiority and power over others.

I hear my words and I cannot believe that I am asked to write of this now, for religion is not one of my strong points, so many divisions I see being created, and instead of beliefs based on only love, there are so many who have used and still do use religion to create division. It doesn't matter to me what belief systems people have, it is their pathway, and all are equally valued by God. This is an experiential world we have called into existence, and there are no rights or wrongs to life except where one closes off love, and if one starts to use ego and self importance to place others under constrictive energies.

I love all beings, all of creation, and no matter where people are with their evolution, one thing is for sure, we need now to defend God's Light! Some would say, "God is the ultimate power, why would God need protection, this is ridiculous", but I am not speaking in human terms. I am speaking of creation itself at risk, for energies which rebel and pull against Gods light and creation are there to defile the very energy which created it, and is there reason to be concerned.

I have total love of God and all of creation, and I honour freewill, but not when it comes to defying God's creation. I was asked to write today of something my soul needed to be revealed, so I am now saying please defend the light now the only way possible, by loving through all situations which will come about, and there will be many events and situations which necessitate us holding love and generating it out, not to force, just to maintain Gods Light in all things. So many events will come, I have been told and shown in the coming years, so many challenges will come to free will and how we use this, and the problem is darkness, negativity tries to constrict, to repress and hold down, and kill beauty, love and the feminine, for in all of creation God loves the feminine, for it is in its purity of creation an energy of nurturing love.

I may sound to some as one who has an idea that is religious in its overtones. No! But I have had many lifetimes defending the Light and seeing the damage done to femininity along the way. In my life times revealed to be me by Lord Melchizedek, Jesus Christ and the Hierarchy, I have worked with them and have chosen now to come to aid Lord Melchizedek to maintain God's Light on earth.

How, by simply and as gently as possible resisting fear and darkness, and reflecting back only love. I am qualified I am told to speak of love as given by God in the beginning, and it is with trepidation I speak of this time coming when religion will be used by powers not of light to hold power over mankind, but also all of creation, and in that I will stand up and say, "I love my Creator - being of all Light, and with all of my being I support God, and will maintain a feminine light", and I hope all of you who read this message allow this into your consciousness now, that it is time to defend God's Light whatever belief system you have, and to do this by loving.

It is such a small thing to ask, but can I do so now, plea for love of God to be returned, the Creator needs you home; all of little ones now.

Let it be done in love!
Virginia

AUSTRALIA, A LAND OF HOPE OR A LAND GOVERNED BY FEAR?

In a world so full of abundance is it so impossible to equate the needs of the general populace with fair play? In this world I know and love I have seen great leaps forward, some explosive moves to change radically the world in a beneficial way so that equality is there foremost in our thinking, but it seems one step forward and two steps back is also the pattern to be achieved by a conforming insular society, but in all this where is fair play?

Who looks after the refugees and the environment?

Can it be said that love abounds now in Australia, or has a deep regard for the welfare of other beings been supplanted with fear once again? An election looming, with both parties having disregard for those suffering the ravages of being displaced; to call them refugees, asylum seekers, and our cure as a nation for this 'disease' is to cancel any good will built up to try to ease the burden of these long suffering people.

There is a place for caution in some circumstances, but what party which considers themselves worthy, or a political leader who is worthy of a governing a country can close the heart and feed fear based ideologies of exclusion? Oh the Christ I know would not say send them off-shore for someone else to deal with.

What we have gained under Kevin Rudd in my opinion has been lost to fear based politics. Are we such a weak minded nation we have not enough compassion to include those suffering, and what of the environment? It is now taken and placed on the back burner so to speak, a clear victory for the mining magnets and oil exploration companies.

Perhaps as voters we should negotiate a new way of looking at life with an open hearted policy to refugees, and be more compassionate, and also see that one day we may because of climate change and environmental disasters be those very people seeking compassion and help from other countries, and will we be turned away without hope or compassion for our plight?

Isn't this the time to say as people of good conscience we abhor such narrow politics, and seek to teach politicians that to shelter in fear from making bold and wise decisions to save the environment is not the way forward?

I consider it my responsibility to stand up for the environment and say to any party or individual who promotes fear based thinking, to move aside and allow someone with deep regard for human rights and the welfare of the planet to take power and govern with clear conscience they are upholding goodness and what is right for future generations.

It is time to change our way of thinking to that of love and compassion. What is of great concern to me is the preaching of religious opinion using religion to gain votes whilst condemning anyone to live life in an impoverished way. Love is the only way forward.

Let us start a movement of love, call it hope, and begin the shape the world with a new view of life, one of openness and grace. Let Australia set the standard for other countries to follow, one of responsibility for all life, and the planet we live upon.

Blessings
Virginia

SOMALIA – GLOBAL UPHEAVAL - FROM THE FEMININE ASPECT

Love that most gentle of energies flows now to heal and harness expressions of compassion for all those significant souls who suffer the ravages of drought in Africa. In Somalia a world tragedy takes place, one which tears at the very fabric of human existence. It is my time to write, to voice the human expression of love given form through the feminine essence, and it is in this deep ache within my being that I feel sorrow, but also so much compassion for those who those brave souls who chose to incarnate at this dramatic time in human history.

A compression of energies takes place around the world, economic upset and some countries verging on recession. At such a time it is so easy to hold on so tightly out of fear so that little money or food can be found to help others, but you know I have faith in you humanity that love will show you the very connectedness to life, and the integration of life.

Whatever occurs on one side of the world very much influences the whole. It is in an expression of love and hope I say this day; the feminine energies, that love within all beings begins to resonate from compassion. Lord Melchizedek said many times we are accountable, responsible, for this world we live upon, but throughout the ages a hardening of attitudes developed where masculine dominance came through, 'the tough will survive', 'survival of the fittest' imbedded within the psyche of humanity, and a soft word of love now issues from me now, not a shout from the rooftops, a compassionate embrace through words to open your heart and show you that softness has great power.

One does not need to formulate fearful acts or fear based projections of world affairs to drawer attention to a situation which affects all. While one soul suffers anywhere upon this planet all are impacted upon. Oh we could turn a blind eye and say, 'economic hardship in my town, in my country means we shut down and become protective', but how is this having faith that openness and love can ease situations?

Lord Melchizedek asked me to write to complement his words, and to give at times a noted view of problematic circumstances, but I will do this in my way, the way of the feminine, and issue love and non judgment, but also strong words when needed, for the feminine is anything but weak.

Tolerance of situations has unfortunately been forced upon femininity in so many ways, and one could say we would have to fight for recognition, to seek to shout louder than men to get attention and be recognized. I am not going down that path, it is the way of masculinity, but I will say with firmness now that this world we live on is now experiencing intense pain; and I wish I could say it will be better – that all one has do is sit and meditate upon peace, but in truth action is needed, and it is needed now as a matter of urgency to aid all those millions of displaced people, to feed the starving masses, and to allow love and compassion to seep through all countries with such a burst of love that shakes energies into love. When love enters and holds a space then the Spiritual Hierarchy can intercede on our behalf. Without love on mass, without significant sacrifice and love shown to those in need the Hierarchies hands are tied.

Human conditions come in cycles, but even a fool has to start to look at the growing climate events, spontaneous areas of extreme damage as a significant sign something needs correcting, and to look at humanity's role in the creation of these environmental disasters.

Love is gentle, but make no mistake the feminine aspect has always held an energy for love and hope to seep throughout humanity. Overly masculine energies now begin to smother this planet in aggression, in war like tendencies, and with hardness, a self protection mechanism.

I could speak as Lord Melchizedek does of the great rift between the rich and poor, or I can say we are of one body you and I, the very soul you are is one with every soul in Africa, or Pakistan, or Bahrain or countless places where heartlessness and aggression has taken hold.

There is such power in love - you are the vessel through which God experiences life on earth, and it is it in your experiences, in your ability to get past old thought patterns humanity evolves, but also of God - Creator of all experiences how close we are to returning home to love, or how distant we become.

We shine each one of us, and every soul upon this planet and beyond is loved equally. No one more important than any other, and it is in this time we are asked to show our Godlike nature, to reach out to the starving, or the homeless, and say, 'yes I can spare this much of food, or cloths, or human effort to aid our brothers and sisters'. You and I are about to embark on an intimate journey to find and move into God's loving energies, and we do this through love.

Many of the conditions now upon earth are of our own making, and we through compassion can reach out and touch others and therein honour God.

Of all the discussions Lord Melchizedek has had with me one aspect is stronger than any other; the need for compassion and love to flow. He has spoken about male dominance in human affairs and coming problems, political, and religious, and the problem with male dominance even in the example set along the passageway of time with the Spiritual Hierarchy sending male avatars, predominantly male spiritual leaders, and thus exacerbating the problem. He spoke at times of the difficulty of revealing truths to a humanity throughout history too ignorant or not evolved enough to listen to words from a woman, and in time this has not helped humanity evolve back to balance.

So it is he has asked me now after many years of finding my power; to take his words for him, and give the feminine aspect into the Melchizedek Order or the Order of Melchizedek, and with time write a set of twelve journals, "From Feminine Aspect" along with female Masters and the Goddesses to now restore balance back to humanity.

I am given his words and blessings to speak at times on his behalf, but also to give words explaining energy changes and how these will impact, and it is in this capacity I write now to take back some of the power taken from the feminine over time.

I will in future books give words of explanation also of the lives of Jesus Christ and Miriam, of King David and his Bathsheba, Akhenaton and Nefertiti, and in each case there was an attempt to honour and restore power back to the feminine, and in each case the feminine was defiled, or denied her rightful roll to deliver equal words of power. It is through these great aspects this knowledge will flow, but my principal job now is to write and guide those open to my words through the troubled times, and it is with a great deal of love I invite you now to become the hope for this world, one we created, and we can now recreate!

Of the years ahead I have been shown a great deal, visions and given words also to aid me understand our human potentials, our ability to do great deeds, and empower the recreation process and ascension energies, or we can draw down energies and experience fear driven beliefs and closed hearted practices, and thereby draw the veil down, so Gods Hierarchy, Archangels, Angels and Masters are restricted to just watching the free will impact of our actions.

Love, compassion and goodness can change the world. Never see love as powerless, or yourself as powerless. You are an aspect of God, somewhat distant perhaps for a time, but nevertheless an aspect of divinity. Our divinity is now being tested to see how we handle situations we as a whole have created.

Love is the key ingredient, and such a powerful one at that. I love my Creator as I love all life - nature and Mother Earth, we, all those souls with which you share the earth need your help, and connection now to love.

Can you help please these souls who are now crying out! "Why has God done this to me"? Not realizing this was manmade, and that man can change these twelve years into years where love is honoured, and the feminine is restored to her rightful place of the right hand of God, and in these days of change and turmoil, I also will aid Lord Melchizedek and offer you my love, a substantial love powered by God. And it is your right also as creator of reality to reach out and become something so much greater, balanced, and in the process restore balance back to the whole. Love is here to stay if the heart stays open, and no one can take our power away. No one! If the heart stays open.

Circumstances may come to try us, but it's all good, we can turn all around just by loving. I stand counted, I will stand with Lord Melchizedek as I hope you will too, and be accountable for actions; and try where possible to make them come only from love. It is in love this is written as a gift to you that you may also know how loved you are.

May you bless life, and life bless you in return.
Virginia

A MINING BOOM, AFTER BOOM COMES BUST – GAS FRACTURING.

Evidence would show the pathway forward for humanity is paved not with gold, but with a broken earth as evidence of mankind's greed. So long we the human race have existed, but not truly out of selfishness we sought new Technologies, and rapid expansion shows a new path is needed of exploration of future technologies, but what a price this planet now pays for the greed for resources. A resource boom it is said stabilizes fragile economies; and holds the world in a place of opportunity, but for what? What future does the human race have if this total lack of concern continues for impactful mining on such a large scale?

Gas fracturing I would like to speak of now, not as an expert to quote figures, but as a concerned citizen of this planet that greed extinguishes now all common sense. The use of gas fracturing begins to pollute underground water, leaching into river systems; land becomes honeycombed with subs structure soils removed and depleted, and poisons used in the process.

I come from a long line of souls who incarnated at this time to help bring positive change, to put forward truth, and to challenge when humanity is becoming the fastest destroyer of life on this planet. We as humanity open mine large areas, polluted still with coal mining; and rejoice when the economy benefits from the mining boom, but after boom comes bust, or the possibility of such. Broken land, broken promises, broken dreams - farmers with rights removed so governments can promote such a boom with little real sort of the consequences.

Of all the subjects now which borders on the obscene for the blatant opportunism and greed, it is this gluttonous rampage through nature.

I put forward my view, a personal view, and a feminine view of life seeing potentials for a dramatic event to come to remind humanity that when all consideration is given over to greed, an imbalance comes. A responsibility for such wide spread damage rests with companies, stockholders and governments, and those who out of lack of concern simply let all slide. Short term thinking can bring long term woes which cannot be repaired, whole systems damaged, ecosystems corrupted and poisoned, and species threatened.

Lord Melchizedek asked me to write of this subject because he like me saw a threat developing, and the implications of this global rampage across the environment now pulls up to a crescendo, but the damage bill to water systems poisoned - rivers and the barrier reef and other areas of gross abuse will come back, action = reaction.

I will simply say I weep for Mother Earth, I see such damage and I weep, but anger is there that complacency on behalf of the general population allows this global greed to continue. Not so! I am told this now comes to a head, warnings do not stop the corruption, only global action and awareness of change as needed, and this is one area I will leave to Lord Melchizedek. Awareness is my area, and awakening those open to change - a flowing energy spreads throughout the world, a mass movement against greed, but it has not even begun to shift on mass, but it will. A global awakening will now come fueled by an awareness of love for truth, and the ethical treatment of the planet and people.

No longer will systems be allowed to run without challenge, now is the time for removal of greed, a cleansing out of all systems of abuse, and over exploitation of people and the earth, and it is powered by love. Love for an ailing planet, but more so a love of truth, and recognition we cannot live for long upon a planet destroyed by our own collective greed.

So it comes now, a period of extremes of energy, of confrontation of darkness in all sectors of society powerless, of individuals fighting to protect their land will now spread, and out of harmony and oneness an allied movement comes to remind governments anywhere that exploitation will no longer be accepted!

So it is this energy flows, an awareness our time to redress wrongs is short. Love can show the way as the United Force for change. A call comes, "no more will we tolerate exportation, fairness and responsibility for actions is called into play.

It will be in a movement it comes, underground waters show depleted use due to poisons callously added, and a responsibility will be called into action to cease such operations.

Blessings.
Virginia

AMERICA - A PLEA –

SUPPORT BARACK OBAMA –

LET HIS WISDOM AND LIGHT SHINE.

The governing force for change now becomes obvious as light is generated within the heart of individuals and nations alike. Within the problematic times ahead one man shines out as of enlightened stance, and with a gentle but powerful appreciation of humanities plight he gathers those who have the ability to heal, but world economies now experience a sharp decline, and to decree a President not fit to hold office after such a short time afforded him to correct economic problems affecting America; seems to be not only illogical, but unfortunate.

Lord Melchizedek granted me the opportunity to speak; when my heart and soul spoke of troubles ahead if a certain course of action was not taken. I choose to speak on behalf of Barack Obama, and beseech the American people to not place unfair burden upon one President when problems have been created over many years and several presidencies.

I have been shown the world situations and possible choices and courses humanity may take, and this course was shown as needed, to have at the helm a captain or President fit for the times ahead, one of wisdom and grace, a President * "of the people, by the people and for the people". Barack Obama has a job to do, and one president cannot be held responsible for a state of decline worldwide of stock markets, and related banking and manufacturing defaulting and inability to manage economic wealth with wisdom.

American now has now a man who can give at last the light and leadership the world needs, and a very crucial time. One term in office is not enough for this man to repair a broken system of monetary regulation and blatant opportunism and greed by individuals, markets and companies. The world will continue to experience financial difficulties until greed and selfish attitudes of regulators of stock markets and banking system ceases.

Many people suffer; it is foolish to push forward with a system which no longer works. The world is now undergoing a cleansing, a clearing out of systems which no longer work, and do not serve to better humanity. America like other countries suffers job losses and economic hardship, but I like Lord Melchizedek urge you to support Barack Obama, he is one man who can pull world and America through some very potentially difficult times, and it is to him do I say. "Hold the Light high, and promote fairness, truth and justice, this is what the world needs now and in the years to come".

Oh many politicians strike a pose for the role, but is it wise to vote in a President who does not have the ethical ideals and skills to maneuver America out of decline? Better perhaps to speak of supporting, and rather than party politics pulling and tugging at policies and taking power, perhaps economies might heal with less ego strutting and honest concern for the nation, for people who are suffering, who do need medical assistance, support, housing and food.

A compassionate nation would say, "let us put aside party politics and divisive measures; to ensure positive action moves America and the world forward. Now is the time to support this man, one who came before at another time in history to help formulate a nation's direction, he did it once as Abraham Lincoln, give him a chance to move you forward with support, pull together, let love guide your actions and votes, not fear and politics governed by fear.

I have seen possible futures we as humanity can create, and we will need wise and noble leaders, those able to put aside the ego, and see the greater good served. Health Care should not be a reason to vote and pull down a politician, this speaks of vested interests to want to maintain even greater riches for the wealthy while people suffer - have no Health Care, and are left to fend for themselves. It is time to see how the world evolves now, across the world with so many holding onto fear, and corruption goes on unfettered.

The world needs a wise and noble leader and leaders, and America has one now! Please do not waste an opportunity to give your people a positive leader at the right time; a time of great need. This is my hope, and I like so many would love to see Barack Obama given a chance to resurrect a very over militarized and impoverished country. Do not blame him for the excesses of others, or decisions made in the past which influence its current economic circumstances.

The world needs hope, support Barack Obama, this was a plea from Lord Melchizedek last year, and I repeat this now, he is so needed to be that Light which shines, and it is my wish he has that chance.

Blessings.
Virginia.

These wise words were once spoken by Abraham Lincoln and are embedded in history as the words of a wise leader.
* *"that this nation, under God, shall have a new birth of freedom -- and that government of the people, by the people, for the people, shall not perish from the earth".*

Perhaps America could listen to the wisdom issued by that same soul Barack Obama here to lead America out of trial, give him a chance to complete his duties.
* From the Gettysburg Address included here as a reminder.

Gettysburg, Pennsylvania

"Four score and seven years ago our fathers brought forth on this continent, a new nation, conceived in Liberty, and dedicated to the proposition that all men are created equal.

Now we are engaged in a great civil war, testing whether that nation, or any nation so conceived and so dedicated, can long endure. We are met on a great battle-field of that war. We have come to dedicate a portion of that field, as a final resting place for those who here gave their lives that

that nation might live. It is altogether fitting and proper that we should do this.

But, in a larger sense, we can not dedicate -- we can not consecrate -- we can not hallow -- this ground. The brave men, living and dead, who struggled here, have consecrated it, far above our poor power to add or detract. The world will little note, nor long remember what we say here, but it can never forget what they did here. It is for us the living, rather, to be dedicated here to the unfinished work which they who fought here have thus far so nobly advanced. It is rather for us to be here dedicated to the great task remaining before us -- that from these honored dead we take increased devotion to that cause for which they gave the last full measure of devotion -- that we here highly resolve that these dead shall not have died in vain -- that this nation, under God, shall have a new birth of freedom -- and that government of the people, by the people, for the people, shall not perish from the earth."

3 HOPE

THE WORLD NEEDS HOPE.

Hope comes to those who have faith in God, but can I be one who speaks now of personal responsibility for your place in the world, a planet now in a state of rapid change. It is logical to believe that climate change is there as a cycle of nature, it is abnormal to believe and in fact irresponsible to believe mankind has not altered the status quo, the equilibrium of this planets ecosystems, and Beloveds to my mind only the irresponsible would continue to turn a blind eye to the present trends beginning to show, of larger than normal earthquakes, tsunamis, snowfalls, blizzards storms, cyclones etc, to do so opens the door for much larger set of events, but I am asking of you this, that you take responsibility for your own actions and dereliction of care of this magnificent water world called Earth.

Chosen people come to Earth now to show a pathway forward, but it can do little good to aid you constantly if efforts are not made to change your ways. We could stand back and let all unfold with climate events and not try to aid you, but not only human beings suffer, innocent creatures do also. Across the globe there is a widening of the number of species becoming extinct, and one could say "I can't do anything about this" but in reality you can!

I have asked my beloved vessel to place messages of warnings of potential events, not to add fear, just to point out the truth is human kind are the creators of much of the suffering which will take place, and all of humanity have a responsibility for their actions.

Oh Beloveds, how easy it would be to live life and turn a blind eye to potentials, especially those which do not impact upon you, but in reality every day around the world areas of land undergo a massive upheaval of one sort or another. Every day now climate events becomes stronger, of greater intensity, and they are created largely by people, some ignorant to the damage created by actions, and others out of greed and a need for more, to have and take more, but I am not here now through this vessel to give a lecture, but to give a direction. As you see events start to flow with the ever increasing damage and ferocity start to look to your actions and change them, and as an active creator being, create positive change; use your voice, your actions to prompt those who do not take personal responsibility for the Earth, Gaia, to do so.

A pretense of ignorance of responsibility does not hold water as they say; to plead ignorance upon leaving this realm everyone will have to account for their actions or lack of them. This is a schoolroom yes, but you humanity are creators, and at the moment on the wrong track. I am not here to give a rap over the knuckles, you have free will, but I will state this very clearly. To ignore what is taking place in other countries, to ignore environmental damage and to see others can correct this, or take care of those suffering will bring to you a reminder, a reflection of what compassion and understanding is, and where personal responsibility is.

Oh my children, to live and not love all life is somehow so sad how some do exist with potentials never utilized, and never seeing they are creator Gods. I have asked my beloved vessel to add these words to aid you, to help you see the writing is not on the wall so to speak. Future events can change with actions, but for politicians to be speaking about climate change and to changes to emission quotas not being implemented until the year 2020 or 2050 is far too late!

I cannot put it any other way except in plain language; YOU HAVE FIVE YEARS TO CORRECT YOUR DAMAGE, LESS EVEN THAN THAT IF PRESENT TRENDS CONTINUE. We will aid you through this, but you as humanity must take the lead, and restructure your belief systems to incorporate love for the planet and all of creation, all creatures, and live with respect and harmony for all life.

You enter this gateway of opportunity, a chosen pathway of opportunity awaits you where *HOPE is needed, but as creators of the destruction worldwide you are also able to initiate a movement of *HOPE, with aware human beings starting to calibrate the needs of societies, localities and countries in the event not only of climate change, but also the results of a worldwide struggle for freedom which will leave many people in need of a home and a country. *HOPE can be that energy you generate now, which will have the positive counteracting power to ease the way for those suffering.

*HOPE springs forth from the thoughts of those fixed in love, and planted into fertile ground of compassion. Planning is needed and a gentle suggestion possibly given to help authorities to see the public can all contribute. Volunteers worldwide when prepared and organized can be the salve all wounds need to recover and it will be needed.

I have asked Virginia to place a list of possible strategies which could be implicated in each locality, and variant to conditions specifically unique to each country, variations and ideas can come from you awakened human beings to see this need. (This along with an explanation of HOPE is included in the Goddess Awareness website under HOPE) *Hope is offered and empowered by God, but also enacted by those earth angels so to speak, all of you who are prepared to be the forward ranks of God's army so to speak.

*Hope is needed for the times to come, through people like you beginning a movement of such profound love it spreads its magic, and no love is ever wasted. If forward planning in one area is not needed through events, then pay it forward, reach out and help other localities, other people at threat, or who are in need, and please be compassionate to those made refugees, they too like you are God's children and so loved.

Be that insightful being who loves life enough to give of yourself and create and empower *HOPE whenever you may live.

My blessings to you.
Lord Melchizedek

HOPE STARTS WITH YOU.

Hope graces all life with opportunities to see beyond present limitations. Hope gives joy and a feeling of comfort that something greater is coming. Hope gives us all the opportunity to see seize the moment and propel energies forward by active participation. Hope is needed now in a world of such beauty, but so much man made trial. Within the human being is the capacity to transcend the myopic view of only that which confronts us now as all important, and allows the world to open up to see a bigger view of life with potentials, but hope is not a static thing. Hope is active in human participation and interaction, instead of hoping for a miracle to come, we can be the hope the world needs at a time of great blessings, but also major challenges to daily life, and indeed the world at large.

We hope that the future will always bring good fortune and grace, but the reality is all great brave souls who chose to incarnate on earth at this time are here as actors so to speak in this great time of change. We have all chosen to be active players to bring light to the world, and therefore to set out to find ourselves and remember who we are, and help others, or to choose the hardest lesson to pull away from God and find a different path, one of separation. Whichever path we take, one thing is for sure, the world needs hope and we can be that hope all need, even those people who in their pain pull away from God, and create pain for themselves and others.

The reality is this magnificent planet we live on is undergoing great changes, vast and savage at times in the climate upheaval which comes. Climate change is one area we can give hope to people, and put in place active plans to open opportunities for healing. We can when joined together be those selfless souls who commit to setting up circumstances to ease others pain and we can help to orchestrate places to go, people to help in situations. We as an active world community can be the mindful pathway where love is offered freely to all in need.

On speaking locally of this need for hope, the response was, "but there are government agencies, S.E.S, etc. to take care of emergencies". All true, but beyond these agencies we can fill the gap worldwide, and offer to be the human potential for grace and love to wrap around people in their pain. Hope is needed, but there is a rational observation, that as in my local town we haven't had disasters on a wide scale, and some agencies are in place to help people so why bother?

May I explain so this becomes clear, hope is needed because we are entering a time where larger events will come, already across the world economic depression and difficulties have impacted and to continue to cripple millions of people.

Whole economies are on the brink of collapse or extreme difficulties, and climate changes has started to impact, and cause a problem further exacerbating the economic hardships people suffer. There now comes a time when added to this, political upheaval also complicates life worldwide, the need for freedom worldwide, a struggle begins for freedom, a thirst for what the west has experienced, and beginning in the Middle East this movement of freedom begins.

Worldwide the struggle for freedom marches on and in its wake pain and some tragic results follow, as well as those of joy, but the reality of this thirst for freedom is worldwide millions of people are potentially going to be made homeless, and without a homeland to call their own. Refugees: always on the lips of politicians will now become a wave of humanity looking for safe harbor so to speak, and there is no single government agency which can look at this problem, and put in place a way forward, to give hope to those in distress.

Worldwide hope is needed, not just another government agency, but the active participation of people like you who love life and freedom, but also value life, all life, and others rights to be comforted and loved through the times to come.

Hope is the active ingredient we can give people by preparing a way forward, locally and on a larger scale to see the heart is kept open, to make sure that closed hearted policies do not take over. We can offer love and increase awareness of people's needs, even within localities. Hope can give people a sense they have worth and are loved, and isn't that what we all seek?

We are becoming something greater, we can evolve beyond the self centered societies which keep others out or trapped in these situations, and we can remind politicians that this is not the time to close down the heart, but it takes people like you who are capable of seeing more than is now obvious in a world gripped by change.

We can help the world to transcend this time of trial and pain and become something so much greater, to become the brotherhood and sisterhood of man, but it needs to start somewhere, and it needs you to be the active ingredient!

Hope springs forth in the strangest of places if the heart of even one person is open enough, and gathered together with others we can move mountains, and pull humanity through future events. Hope doesn't have to be a complicated organization, just concerned people joining their energies, and saying no I want the world to be a better place.

Be the glue that holds the world together, and start by talking to others about what is needed on the local front. How can volunteers help? If people have skills these can be offered freely, without ego or ownership, let your soul speak and tell you what is needed, and simply aid this vision to fall into place.

We will add ideas or ways you can organize help here, how to collect information about what is available locally.

Hope is you, it starts with your attention being drawn to the problems people suffer, and it helps by putting ideas, strategies in place to help and coordinate with the existing organizations, to bridge the gap, and to let these dedicated organizations know you are not trying to take the job, but be part of the solution.

As it stands now Australian has had a set of environmental circumstances which should now start to make people see that hope is needed in every town, in every state and locality, and on mass we can be the loving volunteers who can aid in emergencies, and it is needed now.

If you feel you're heart is open and these words ring true, then it is time to begin. Start by getting together with others, talk about where the problems are in your locality, state and region, and begin to love life enough to reach out with your own essence of love and efforts. Love is needed and non judgment because along the way you will be confronted by people who are not open to loving inclusion of others' needs and sadly there is a fear of refugees.

Go forward anyway, love anyway, and pushed past barriers, but in a loving way, but please make it happen!

In Profound Peace
Virginia

HOPE MISSION STATEMENT:
Hope – On – Planet – Earth.
Helping – Organise – Plan – Execute

Introductory Mission Statement:

We live in a world becoming more isolated and distant, and many people never knowing their next door neighbour let alone caring for strangers. The world we live in becomes less tolerant and loving, and it is time to change all that. We have an opportunity to begin a movement of love and caring which can begin locally and spread to heal an insular world, and make life richer for everyone. Can we dream of a better world where love flows freely to heal people in times of trial, where situations are beyond their control, yes I believe we can.

In this vision people are kinder, more caring, and they look after each other as valuable beings who are worthy of respect and love. We can all be dreamers with a greater vision!

What I see is already there, the potential, we just need to find a way of starting this movement of love and compassion. It's more a way of living, compassionate living, and it doesn't need rules or laws or dogma to start with, it is a philosophy, people just opening the heart and reaching out to see we are all interrelated so to speak, all one, and what affects any member of society, or for that matter the planet, affects us all - **H.O.P.E.** is but a single movement of love and understanding, and it may seem so impossible a concept to begin with, but it isn't.

Any movement of love must at somewhere, why not here, with us, people who can hold a bigger vision, of a world needing just such love as does flow from an open heart.

The Potential for Climate Catastrophe is worldwide.
There is not a country which is not exposed to the potential damage from natural or climate change catastrophes.

- Recently there was major concern for the safety of countries around the Pacific Ocean, eventuating from the affects of the tsunami from the Japan earthquake. This unpredictable tsunami threatened most of these Pacific Ocean countries. A threat on one side of the world can impact far and wide, we are truly a global community interlinked in many ways, and climate change, plate tectonics etc unites us all.

Where can this start? It can start by looking at what people need, and in emergency situations there are so many ways loving support can help.

So let us now start with this situation:

Climate change though debated by some has a very real impact upon people, violent storms, bushfires, earthquakes, tsunami's, flooding and the aftermath of these such as contamination, potential radiation from disasters as we have sadly found recently. Lives can be lost, homes destroyed, people displaced and thrown into chaos, and it can happen at any time, to anyone.

So perhaps one way we all could help is to be that vehicle for help to come to people in need. We can provide information resourced from Agencies, Departments, Councils, groups etc, to eliminate confusion, and we can find those areas not yet perceived by authorities, and fill that gap giving information to the public. With bureaucracy and Government Departments often people's needs falls between the cracks, and in the exploration of statistics and facts the loving component is lost, people become merely statistics after the event.

You can be part of the solution by:

- Put the philosophy of **H.O.P.E.** into action in your area:
- Create a register of the elderly, those with disabilities, the infirmed who in emergencies may need help, and provide them with contact details needed (with their permission).
- Resource supplies and people who are willing to help with situations, volunteers, such as taking in people displaced by climate events or other situations. There is so much we can all do to aid people, and to dispel the isolation which cripples lives.

GETTING H.O.P.E. STARTED:

Out in the world there are millions of people who would help if they just had a pointer about what to do and how to do it - volunteers, but first it takes organisers, people with vision and a big heart to see beyond the 'it's too hard, too big aspect, and where do we start'? Any really worthwhile movement or group has to start somewhere, and the place to start is here, by deciding firstly, 'Do we care about helping people, and to create a better world'? I hope the answer is yes.

We can change the world by starting at home, getting to know the neighbours', seeing beyond our own needs, isn't that what community is all about and isn't the world one much larger community?

Reach out to others even if some do not appreciate the gesture! Remember a smile speaks a thousand words.

H.O.P.E. is offering just that, hope to people who see no hope, where life or situations have become so difficult, and this vision is multidimensional, it can start with simply starting a campaign to get to know your neighbours, your street, to reach out and say, 'Hello, if you need me I am here'.

H.O.P.E. is a movement of open hearted love and compassion, and it is sorely needed in a world which is becoming so hardened to the plight of others, and it can start here with you now.

Let us look at ways and on what levels you can participate.

- What can be done in your Local community?
- What can be done around the world to help people in need?
- How to awaken people?
- What resources' are needed?
- How to let people know how they can help?

Working with existing Agencies and others.

Some may say, "but there are other agencies which cope with emergencies situations", true, and **H.O.P.E.** is not trying to usurp their jobs or in any way undermine their directives and work, but merely coordinate, gather information, and make it available to the public, and to fill any gaps and create an awareness of potential problems not already covered. We have approached various councils for evacuation plans, for emergency strategies and information and found this generally not available, hard to find the person with information, or given the run around. Imagine then the scenario in periods of panic for the public to have to chase around looking for a person, information and help or the departments are not open at that hour. Sometimes these Councils need prompting that information is lacking (we found this in all but one council that was contacted locally.)

Australia, unlike many other countries has been spared much of the earth upheaval and climatic events to date, but more and more we cannot count on being the lucky country and in escaping disasters. Sadly the Victorian bushfires, Queensland and Victorian Floods, Queensland, NT and WA Cyclones and inland Tsunami taught us many lessons in unpreparedness, and this is a luxury we cannot afford, to be complacent any longer: the thought that events or disasters are always in someone else's backyard is a thing of the past. We are at an impactful time, one of waiting for events to come, and then saying, 'we could do more as a community'. There are wonderful people in emergency groups, R.F.S, S.E.S and others, and there is a need for those organisations to have more help, but there is also a need for more, for love and compassion to fill in the gaps which are created.

It is of concern that many people are disconnected from the plight of others if it doesn't impact upon them, but let's start to move humanity back into the loving zone, but now to the nuts and bolts so to speak.

We invite your participation, ideas and feedback. Let's start this with the following questions:

- How do we/you begin this?
- Where do we/you go from here?
- What can you offer of your own energy to make this happen?
- How can this be implemented when looking at the bigger picture (worldwide)? Act locally, think globally!
- How do we/you start a movement or group to reach people in need, what can we/you offer?
- How can we raise funds for advertising, if considered necessary?
- Are we prepared to put ourselves out for the greater good?

This is a question. Is love enough, I think it is! Let us make this happen! We need your help.

We invite your participation, wherever you are around the world, if you would like to add your feedback, suggestions, or offer help please contact us by emailing: wingsinc@dodo.com.au .

HOPE - THE NEW ENERGY OF THE AGE.

A remembrance comes of love as shown to me by others who also struggle with life, and there can be no greater joy than that of expressions of love and compassion shown, felt, and sent on in loving gestures, a flowing of love from one heart to another. So much love truly exists in this world, at first glance one could be forgiven for seeing only the unseemly, those acts of foolishness from the many who do not truly see and feel God's love and abundance flowing through them.

I am given an opportunity to write about a subject so very dearly needed in many areas of the world, from third world countries, to those countries where abundance and commercialism reigns supreme. Hope is needed everywhere, but what truly is hope? Can it be a mythological magical ingredient not known to us and therefore out of reach. Oh No!

It is the very substance of love made manifest by gracious deeds, and opening a dialogue, a portal through which compassion is the dominant energy. Love bleeds with such compassion at times: this extraordinary energy permeates the very air and extends out much like an invisible mist.

Hope is the structural form of this loving mist of dual purpose, to open the hearts of those suffering, and the very healing balm which extends its energy into areas of great despair, and says softly, trust again; open the heart and mind and breathe in this indefinable energy of optimism. Hope is love made available through wishing, drawing to you the softer, gentler energies which expel fear and despair.

Hope can be the energy the world now creates, generates and broadcasts out to counteract every form of aggression and ugliness, corruption and despair. What can hope to do? A great deal because hope is a pure gesture aimed at the heart of God, and God is ever listening to his little ones! Hope is his inner whispering given form, a way for those who are at their last end – grasping hold of love and calling out in desperation with words or thoughts, and God does listen, and through his extended energies - us works wonders. Not always will that offering come immediately, but hope is the instrument through which love is drawn to aid the dispossessed and poor, the suppressed, and those lost without love.

I am given a great blessing to be asked to write from the heart and help create in you, in everyone, that opening of the heart which brings a flood of love and compassion for all beings, and this is so very needed! Love flows, always, it is just a matter of us being aware and open enough to feel it, and some may say it's easy for her to say, she does not suffer as we do, but I have in my various lifetimes and have prepared by learning all forms of experience to test, to remember who I am, and to fully aid others in also seeing the power and beauty of God, and please believe me in this when I say I am just as soul like you doing it the hard way on earth, in a state of awakening.

Slowly remembering my Source, my Creator and yours! I could recount many lifetimes of violence and repression my soul has suffered upon the journey back to God, and in every lifetime a new degree of remembrance was found. Sometimes I won the battle to reveal more of myself, and others I did not fully stand in my power, and each and every one of them was precious for the experience brought the soul back to God and balance.

It isn't easy in these experiences, in the difficulties and pain we can learn the true reason we are here on earth in body; to let go of the illusions of life, the self created profiles which place us into situations, countries, or places, or with people, asleep, totally cut off from love and therefore God.

To some it may sound so strange to hear a woman speak so of hard times, poverty and struggle, and to say love and power can be found in them, but it is true. We are all valiant souls, brave beyond belief for we choose to tramp across experiences which teach us strength and test our ability to remember who we are, and no it isn't easy at times. It is hard beyond belief for we are subject to others whims and thought patterns, we also are hampered by the very rebellious energies who oppose God and who do not want us to remember who they are, and they certainly do not want you to; because it results in an illusion of a loss of power.

Power is truly only in conditions where the nobility of all mankind develops and grows, where individualism in its astonishing beauty offers a way forward for the whole.

Expansion is found in such abundant love, and it's why heavy energies abound where there are control issues, of those governed by fear.

We can bring to each area around the world a new energy of Hope, an extended energy of love given form, and love breathed into the germinating embryo of an idea. Hope is that gateway, portal through which a wind of profound love can flow out into all the loveless darkened corners, all those places of despair, but how can this occur if not by us in a joint expansion of love and faith in God and ourselves upholding a higher vision. We can create it as co-creators with God, and saying no we have had enough of a world driven by blatant commercialism without love, of dictatorships gained by fear, not love!

Today we stand at a gateway of opportunity, to hit out on a new course for humanity. A movement of Hope, and what is hope but love put into action people like us seeing opportunities every day, in every sector of society, to make it a better world and shut the door on fear and denial of human rights. We en - mass are the creators. We as powerful beings can say, 'oh I see a situation I can aid with people who are in trouble'. A gesture of love given by another, and then pay it forward. Be that dynamic being who will not let fear stand in the way of the creation process. There are beautiful moments to share, love in all its generous forms leads the way, and the virtue of generosity of spirit cannot be overstated.

For some Hope is a lost cause, but it is not, it is the very way forward. It is truly the true teachings of Jesus Christ, of Buddha, Mohammed, the original concept without man made intrusion, in pure form it is a way of life, of being a generous life of compassion and love and sharing with others, and if you have little give of yourself as those thousands of volunteers in Queensland are doing after the floods, an active remembering of our true heritage, which is true love.

The confines which limit us must go! The constructs of thought and teachings which say, only this person is acceptable to help, to love, and to include. Throw it all out the window and breathe pure air of love, with no limitations on who one can approach and help, befriend and include one's life.

We are pure souls, we are God created beings of infinite power, and we can make a difference! We can and will because we have help from Angelic beings, Ascended Masters, all great beings of pure light are aiding us now, but many in their plight struggle on unable to gain a sense of self love or power because they are limited by one thing, there is no remembrance of their light and the Source, the omnipotent, omnipresence Creator.

Many people do not know they just need to ask; to call out mentally or otherwise and say,' God, I am here help me please', and help will come in some form. All great beings of light must be invited to come into your realm. They are governed by rules of engagement, so if you need help, I ask for it. Say in simple terms, God I need you, your help and you will have light beings rush to your defense. At first you may not be aware of their presence, but situations will change around you and warmth, a feeling of being wrapped in love comes to those who open their hearts. We are all in need of love, there is no soul exempt from that, and the more hearts which open and pour out love and compassion, the stronger the tidal flow of love will be which washes over this planet, reconstructing, breaking away corruption and illusions of separateness.

We live in the most potent time of change, and there is no area positive change cannot reach, but first we need to initiate this energy, and it needs no leaders, no rulers, no rules or constraints other than, 'love one another as I love you', and isn't that the greatest gift of love, to pass it on.

Perhaps Jesus Christ was simply saying, forget the illusions, the institutions and power trips, 'just love one another as I love you', the ultimate statement of Hope. The power phrase to end all statements, and it is open ended, and it empowers all who hear it and heed it.

Hope is the ultimate gift you give the world, a world very much in need of it. Hope is given to the world now and you can carry it and empower it wherever you are. Create a movement of hope, not one of ownership as one says 'this is mine to lead', for this does not empower others and it denies Jesus Christ's original concept. Love cannot be owned, it pours forth constantly from God, Creator of us all.

The concept of Hope now enters into your consciousness, and please promote hope everywhere, speak openly of a new way of life, where there are no barriers to others, where openness and compassion lead the way, and if you meet opposition as you most assuredly will along the way from those who are so closed they cling out a fear to exclusion and hard ways, blow them a kiss and truly mean it, for there is nothing more powerful than love!

It is time we did this now, generate the birth process of Hope, give birth to it, and send it forth into life with love, and then see how the world changes, closed societies, religions, and country's will dissolve and in its place will be a new form of society, one open, expansive and giving and isn't that better, to know what we are here for, and complete this incarnation having achieved a miracle, the birth of a golden age of love empowered by each one of us?

This as truly possible, and I see abundance of Hope now in Australia with whole regions being helped, people leaving their homes and work to unselfishly aid others, for no other reason than love and compassion reigning supreme.

Play it forward people, we are almost there and we all have the part to play with profound love.

Virginia

4 ONENESS

THE HIGHER TEACHINGS OF JESUS CHRIST.

TIME FOR THE RETURN OF THE FLOCK.

Expansion of consciousness comes not from outward words of another, but through inward searching, striving from the higher dimensions expressions of love straight from the sacred heart of God. Such is this time of recapture of truths shown to me via my higher self connection to God, my Father and yours. I am but a soul on the path as all others are, but with an exception, I do remember who I am - my heritage, and I see this is my responsibility to speak of this from my heart connection, given forth this day a pronouncement, love is here to stay!

Upon a path walked a chosen boy, one who shunned authoritarian beliefs which did not empower the whole. He spoke from the heart, but he didn't withhold truth from any, it is my path to follow his footsteps and to pronounce a new way of being according to God. Driven images of old beliefs will fade now, given power no longer from the lower self for all those acknowledging Christ within the heart. It is in opening the sacred heart does knowledge flow now. Within the heart sack area, a sacred heart is held, a spiritual vessel holding life force and energy within it, which only opens to true unconditional love. Christ energy flows from the sacred sac, the beating heart of God.

When gathered in millions souls will be shown by the light, purity and integrity, all enhanced and molded into form which then becomes the garment of perfection, the seamless garment. Such is this time now, our own divine light is needed, but also invited to participate in bringing the flock's home.

Jesus Christ was a man with a mission, to remind each and every person of their true heritage and light, and not to dwell upon the lower aspects, which are beneath his vibration. So it is I give you now into your unconsciousness these teachings- one simple teaching at a time, and you are asked to stop, pause, and contemplate upon the seven layers of meaning in each profound yet simple teaching.

Acknowledging a supreme power has been a problem for many millions of people because they do not yet see their own potential and that of others, we live in a world consumed with self interest, but seldom is there an adventurous soul who puts aside this way of life. Yet they are there, enlightened souls.

Each and every one of them with an understanding, one simple and yet profound truth; love flows from God to all beings equally.

Why is it then humanity has sought to exclude people and segregate them into boxes? I will tell you what I see as the main reason, there is no recognition of the divine spark of light in all people, so perhaps the first place to start with the teachings of Jesus Christ is in the beginning. One simple yet obvious truth, God created all life but with differences, not because some are superior, but because all diversity in life is needed for God to experience creation.

So this is the first teaching. All life is precious. All life, not just some, all were created equal, and this is difficult for people to get their heads around, because we have had it instilled in us that man was given power over the earth and all upon her. This is going to be extremely difficult for some people to understand, that they are not superior to plants, or animals, or people of others colours and religions, but the truth is all life is precious, and God experiences Himself/Herself through each and every person, rock and creature. Reflect upon this please! if God is within the person you gossip about or persecute, or reject as less than you what are you saying to God?

Each of these truths are easy to corroborate, just think about the statement and stop, see God in everyone you touch, everywhere, in those countries where poverty is rife, in rich nations where materialism is out of control, but also in the oceans and a whale. What are we as humanity saying to God when we do not value who we are, and we see ourselves as exclusive and beyond reproach, but others are not? How can God experience creation and feel in any way truly happy that the creation is worthy? Judgments aside when are we going to learn that world events are open to all people, and at any stage there may be events which switch the status quo; climatic events which overthrow economies, and move millions of people into the position of experiencing loss and poverty, to be refugees. At any stage the lessons may be reversed, so we can learn to be more God-like, Christ like and to strive for perfection for all beings.

This is the first higher teaching of Jesus Christ. ALL LIFE IS PRECIOUS! Let us now look at the possible implications of this one teaching.

How can life be precious? Well let us look at how God has designed creation.

All life is a vibrational frequency, a modulation of light and vibration, a geometric matrix which starts as a simple life form, and through variance and geometric wavering of pattern and structure that takes on a form of its own. Each and every one a unique vibration, and in perfection for the placement within creation and how it interacts with all others, and the vibrational frequencies set up a sympathetic resonance which enhances creation. Some forms are short lived, and others take a circuitous pathway of growth and develop patterns of complex natures, but all are reliant upon each other, for without any one of these forms the signature of the universe begins to change, and an imbalance begins. Soon one vibratory field overpowers another, and the harmony is lost. This in a nutshell is where we are now.

We, humanity over the ages have created an illusion of exclusiveness, of a superior attitude to other creatures, nations, religions or people, and it is why we are now asked to look at what we are doing and bring things back into alignment.

I was asked to aid Lord Melchizedek to bring the flocks home, and I questioned, back home to what? Are we all going to leave the earth at once? Are we going to move on mass into a new vibration? No. We are headed into a time of extreme changes, because we as humanity have chosen the course of action. God just wants us to remember who we are and return home to the Creator. Yes many will depart the Earth of their own soul choice, but this is not the reason. We are invited to restructure life as Jesus Christ taught in His time on Earth.

We are invited to start a movement of compassion, and understanding that the complexity of life is at risk. And we are all part of the solution, all of us, a linkage of energies so complex and intricate in our forms and energy we can bring about a planetary awakening, and one where we don't need to be of a particular religion or belief system. This movement will be expansive and not be held back by governments or people of limited thought pattern.

A vast shifting of energy took place where energies began to change, and we are all going home.

For some it will be a transformative shift in consciousness, for others it will be a gentle reminder that we cannot coexist on earth any longer unless we stop and behave in a new way.

We have come to a doorway of opportunity. Where God has felt creations drifting further way, and it is time for a reminder. This reminder for many people will come as a total challenge to their way of living, so they start to see other people as divine and more compassion flows. Many people will simply let go of greed and a need to judge others, and some will choose life threatening climatic upheavals to challenge their humanity and light. Whatever way this comes, all are asked to change and return home to love. It's as simple as that! We can start a movement of caring, be it a small movement on a local front to begin to take care of others, and for some it will be worldwide, a movement back to love. But be aware, often the way our soul chooses to learn is not easy, be heartened by the knowledge you are loved and valued, and what you show God in your behavior and selflessness will definitely aid the whole.

This then is the first teaching, one simple yet profound in its complexity, ALL LIFE IS PRECIOUS. What does this imply? Think about the implications for you, your family and the world at large. Say "I am divine and of God, and I am invited home to an understanding of my complexity, and how much do I have to learn about other people/ life, our planet?

What happens if I choose to ignore this invitation to look at His first teaching?"

The answer, your soul will choose the most appropriate course to learn by, but now all life will begin to resonate to love, and not the self love which is termed greed and selfishness. This love is to put on the invisible garment of divinity and shine a light so bright you lift life experiences for everyone on this planet and beyond.

This is our invitation to come home, and in doing so help others along the way, not so much to ask is it?

Blessings.
Virginia Melchizedek.

FORGIVE THEM FATHER FOR THEY KNOW NOT WHAT THEY DO.

Becomes the catch phrase used to sculpt nations at times of peace and war, for in this time line called life comes a new awareness of the misgivings of many who as they awaken become aware for the first time in their lives that over time many mistruths have been given, but for what purpose? What possible purpose could there be in keeping the masses of humanity in ignorance, save to keep power? But what sort of power, and who could keep this power by suffocation of facts, and further to this add pronouncements over time that they held, acquired, and had total control of truth. But what sort of truth is so powerful that it needs to be told and perpetuated? What is so explosive that control was thought to be needed. Who could hold such knowledge now, and how can this hidden truth be shown?

This is the truth of these times, Jesus Christ held many teachings which were considered to be too explosive, too powerful, so much so that the priesthoods who held religious dominance thought it best to keep and suppress such teachings.

Some with a misguided belief that human consciousness could not handle such high esoteric teachings- some of which were revealed only in Jesus Christ's time only to the elect few, those who showed an elevated consciousness, but can I now speak of this and reveal that which was hidden on so many levels?

Jesus Christ came to show humanity how to live, not how to die! He came to share his insights and his skills, but also to reveal the most potent truth of all. AS ABOVE SO BELOW! Meaning as God created Jesus Christ in His image, he also so loved the world and all of creation the Creator wanted humanity to evolve, and the trouble is that power has been held by religious bodies, those who oversee what is taught, and how it is taught, and it is always far easier to control the crowds with fear than to teach total and unconditional love of each other.

One of the keynote addresses Jesus Christ gave was his address to his disciples, those men and women he chose for their openness of mind and heart. Jesus saw a potential, he in all his clarity saw truth before him. He saw that God did not selectively create one man and say, now go and give your wisdom to the masses, God asked him to reveal by example. His parables were simply worded verses, but underneath each of those parables there were highly evolved truths carefully hidden until the consciousness of man have evolved enough to reveal them.

Was Jesus Christ, Son of God, definitely! Uniquely so, no! just blessed with a vision to share and the gift of clarity and action. He came to teach by example, but to teach what? What is it that humanity had not evolved enough to understand?

He came as a wayfarer to show the way, he reached out on every level to the dispossessed and poor, to the out casts, he held classes equally for his women disciples, not just male disciples, and yet what has been shown or taught? Not that humanity should take Jesus Christ example literally, "to love one another as I love you, to live in harmony with each other and to forgive".

Each and every one of his parables is but a simplified example of a bigger universe. Each and every one unlocking a universal truth, one so powerful that the earth would literally transform and change overnight if everyone was empowered by truth.

Dogma has no place any longer in the metamorphosis of man, it is time humanity returned to the stars and took their rightful place at the right hand of God!

How? By acknowledging the divine heritage which is the divine right of every man, woman and child on this planet and beyond, literally AS ABOVE SO BELOW. All that God is can be revealed by a truly looking inward, but to do this one must first let go of those heavy teachings which were originally given because it was believed humanity could not handle such potent knowledge, and that they must be controlled, and this was so capably done with an emphasis upon the lowly aspects of humanity. Always was it, and in some quarters still emphasized that humanity needed to be governed by fear, a fear of God as number one of the requirements for crowd control. How can this be of benefit? To fear God, when God is omnipresent, omnipotent, and all loving?

God is love and only love, and there is no attachment on God's behalf to our human frailties. It doesn't please God to see humanity kept ignorant of their divine heritage.

I am asked to come at this time and be the reminder of the chosen course for humanity, to lead the flocks home, but when told of this I could not understand how I could add anything to aid with leading the flocks home, but now I see, I just needed to be like so many people, to remember my source, and accept fully my divine right to remember who I am, a daughter of God.

Yes, I dared to say I am a daughter of God, because it is true! Love is the glue which holds us altogether, and instead of revealing we are divine and thereby seeing the divinity in others, we are still lost and lead down a path whereby there is a need to deflect God's children from remembering who they are, and powerfully fitting that image.

How easy it is to grope in the darkness and take a crumb given out as knowledge only given to those who were of a particular belief, or who are granted status as one of those uniquely blessed by way of religion. No! It is time for the cosmic to reclaim all sons and daughters, administrators of a new world, one created by enlightened beings and given power by a direct line to God.

How beautiful will the world be with total recognition of each other as divine beings. Some so lost now in the trappings of religious fervour they are afraid to pronounce divinity within. It is time indeed so that the flocks returned home to a recognition of that false premise that we are without worth, and this amplifying the sinning nature of humans must go. All life evolves, and mankind, or should I say of the brotherhood and sisterhood of light has become something greater.

The title of this passage is called "Forgive them Father for they know not what they do", and refers to those who still hold on so tenaciously to power wrongly gained and at the expense of Jesus Christ. I know that many would think, how dare this woman speak of being a daughter of God, and pronounce it is time to return home to God, to embrace God with all of your heart and soul directly, but it is time the illusion of separation from our Creator was put aside and a greater wisdom was revealed; we are divine!

It is time to reclaim our divine heritage and truly look into our own hearts and find the truth in Jesus Christ teachings. He so loved the world he gave his light, but do not take his example wrongly, he was showing the way to true inner life is to know God with all of our heart and soul, and in that is truth.

He did not come to die, but to show us how to live, without judgment of any, prostitutes, sinners, (though I don't accept this word, but believe it to be a statement used over time by religious authorities for control of the population by fear.) We are all are God created beings, simply here to learn, and sometimes we take what appears to be a wrong turn but it is in fact a self imposed test, a lesson to find out how powerful our ability to overlook all the earth diversions is and to find our way home.

I was asked to lead the flock home, and I agonised over this not believing that I had anything to offer, such is the learning we all tend to gather through life, that only those prescribed by a certain religion or post hold any answers or power. Wrong!

I am asking my Father. 'Please forgive them for they know not what they do', all those who deliberately, subconsciously, or consciously try to keep humanity limited in thinking and beliefs.

It is time for unification of all people. It is time for a

universal shift of consciousness where restrictions, boxes of limited thought patterns are opened, and we all become part of the Cosmic Brotherhood and Sisterhood of Light, all equal, no borders of religion, race, or colour to separate us.

I am a woman with a mission, not some holier than thou mission; just a need to reveal some truths which are strongly there and needing to be told. It is time to remember who we are and come home, to understand the cosmic ramifications of staying rigid and locked into old energies and thought patterns.

The human consciousness evolves now to set humanity free, and so I do say it is time to let the barriers dissolve which bind and enslave human consciousness.

Evolve now, and please remember who you are, and like me say, 'my Father, forgive them for they know not what they do, all those who abuse power, or who try to hold humanity captive, you cannot succeed, God wishes His children to return home', and it will be so!

Blessings
Virginia Melchizedek

ONENESS –
A TIME FOR THE RETURN OF THE FLOCKS

Hopefully we as humanity enter these dramatic years with optimism and hope for a brighter future for all people. How can this optimism be put into practice? Perhaps we could look at our daily lives and surrender the need to see the world only as our oyster, excluding others from such a vision of healing, oneness and prosperity. This is a year of great extremes, of highs and lows and a preponderance of issues to deal with on a human level, but within the scope of each person is a new pathway into oneness.

Oneness is such a concept that seems so very simple, and yet we as humanity still haven't grasped the full concept. We tend on the whole to view the world from our point of view and not see others ideas as acceptable, and yet do you know, I feel that hope is still there as a concept all can bond to, and in fact will bond to as these years proceed leading up to 2012 and beyond. And yes there will be life beyond 2012, but what sort of life depends upon us, for the future rests in our hands.

There was a time long ago when people saw that simplicity and goodness were the real teachings to follow, that of oneness and sharing, and along their way they accumulated little wealth, they gave to those less fortunate and spoke softly of life, but what they did not have was a time of religious acceptance, they had beliefs which did not conform to doctrine set down over time by established religion, and such a sad fate befell these thousands of souls, but also all of those of conventional religious belief of the region, those brave people who allowed their own integrity and judgment to come through at a time of great trial, I am now speaking about the Cathar's and the deep feeling of honouring they created in the people of that area.

What was it that these people preached that caused such hatred and oppressive violence from the church of that time? Perhaps it was that Christ's teachings were only ever meant to be a way of life. How to live a life of goodness and compassion - how to be truly compassionate to others, and so they (the Cathar's) brought about a reformation and protectionism from ordinary people who did uphold beliefs which were ruled by church doctrine, but when challenged those people chose to give up their life to defend these gentle people to allow them to live as they believed they should. It is a credit to those fifty odd thousands people who could put their own religious beliefs on hold to uphold higher principles. The way of the Cathar's and supporters was a violent end, but what it has shown is that goodness and compassion can win out.

There is some discussion about what influenced these people in this area of France. Some have made alluded to the fact that Mary Magdalene went to France after the crucifixion, and spread her teachings, those she shared with Jesus Christ, and I believe there is much truth in that, for these are the basic teachings of Jesus Christ and Miriam (Mary). Their way was not the way of doctrine, but a way of life. They taught how to live with goodness in the heart, oh yes the teachings were simple, but even more relevant today. All the Cathar's believed may not have been of their teachings, (Christ and Miriam) and had developed a distinctive flavour of their own, but the simple truth is hope for a better way of life and compassion and love for all beings was the central viewpoint.

Around 70,000 people died including the Cathar's and those defending the Cathar's beliefs or right to have them, but we really need to ask is, if the Cathar's were around today, has the church evolved enough to see beauty in simple teachings, or have we as humanity not evolved much at all?

I find the simple goodness of the Cathars very appealing because they seem to reflect to me just how far we have come away from the principle of compassionate sharing and goodness, and Miriam and Jesus' teachings.

We are living in a world where religion is about to come to a collision point because there is that rigidness of belief there still where we expect others to bend to our beliefs, and on the whole we do not see that we should give up our luxuries or whims to help others, even if that one we would be helping most is the planet who feeds and nurtures us.

I have come to a time of explanation of my own feelings towards religion, and over the past months I have had to process my own feelings, and it isn't comfortable to see that I still held onto feelings of anger with the way religion has suppressed femininity and truth throughout the ages.

I like so many other people now question any religion which hoards wealth and enforces religious dogma by way of holding people trapped into beliefs which I belief to be contrary to Jesus Christ's teachings. But in my introspection I also saw that some religions have done great good, and helped millions of people along the way, and this must be remembered that some good has come out of the evolution of churches. But my annoyance with the way cultures across the globe have been decimated by religious intolerance cannot be easily overlooked, for I see rigidness there strongly in the inability to let others have their beliefs and not dictate or convey damnation as a punishment for not conforming to dogma, as was so often the case.

Has humanity grown in understanding enough to see the wisdom in that gigantic leaps forward are necessary where the acceptance of others is concerned?"

We are given the advantage these days of having worldwide communication and yet there is such pressure exerted to believe a certain way, in that case where does free will come into it?

I was asked by Lord Melchizedek, the Masters and God my Father, to begin a movement across the globe of Oneness.

Oneness can be taken as exclusiveness, and this is certainly not what the Hierarchy have in mind. Humanity has evolved enough to start to think, to question, and to see that often old dogmas which were included thousands of years ago when humanity was not as evolved, are not as relevant now. But have we evolved to see that Religion can also be a most damaging force if it comes from exclusiveness and judgment of others beliefs.

All religions have merit, once we can get past the doctrine and duplicity of function, if we can see that God never intended that Christianity go the way of discrimination of femininity. In fact I am told by Lord Melchizedek and Jesus Christ that their teachings were only ever love, and simple examples of how to live a life of goodness and compassion, and that is all that is asked of us now, that we question, we see that divisions will not help the world.

It isn't a case of Moslems against Christians; Shiites against Sunnis, there should be no division within the human race.

As humanity we have evolved enough to say, am I prepared to live a conscious life of goodness and caring.

It means so much when you consider the world will encounter problems, and when it comes down to it, we are one!

We have one creator, we are divinely created, and of one energy, why then do we need to divide ourselves up into these groupings? That time of having a superior attitude is over.

The world will present us with reminders that we are one people, all needing to remember our source, and for some people that will be that they do not believe in a Creator at all.

God does not hold petty jealousies and a need for punishing people. God is only love and has acceptance of us in all our uniqueness and whatever level of consciousness we are. God is in all of us, and it is time for the flocks to return home, some literally, some assume a conscious awareness they are of God and therefore divinity created, as is everyone on this planet regardless of religion or lack of it.

It is time to let the barriers drop, and wherever you are around the world begin to start by remembering to live by this one simple teaching, LOVE ONE ANOTHER AS I LOVE YOU. Once the heart opens then love will flow and barriers drop aside. But is time! Time to be all we are, divine, and see that same divinity in others, whatever country, colour or belief system.

I have come to a time of letting go, of shedding preconceived ideas, and I am told the energies now will help all beings to shed and prepare to return home to our creator. The Return of the Flock is quite literally with us now, and it is time to surrender the old, those feelings which keep us apart and prevent us from soaring with the angels, which is our rightful heritage.

Blessings
Virginia Melchizedek

5 ISAAC NEWTON

ENERGETIC ACTIVATION OF THE ORDER OF MELCHIZEDEK BY LORD MACHIVENTA MELCHIZEDEK.

Discussion breeds growth through expansion of consciousness, but many do not understand that within the physical existence they are energy beings, light sources in their own right. Many are so closed within the physical, the material existence little time or effort is given to the soul and life purpose; why you are on earth now. This is the time of reclamation of the human species, to bring them home to their own divine lineage, but during this most important of times many do not see or feel a particular allegiance to the light, but plunder others energies, and all of you who are aware of energy around you now see and feel that you are more than the physical body.

As a scientist in my day I experienced, saw and felt a divine connection, but couldn't quite understand that each person is in miniature an example of the divine.

This discussion is all about energy. How to feel this connection and how to explain it to others. You enter now a period of extreme growth, an energetic alignment of mammoth proportions, for this is the long awaited period of time known by many as the harvesting. It is the time of Melchizedek, and for that reason we do announce that the opening of the Order of Melchizedek has officially taken place and will now function.

It is Lord Melchizedek who holds energy for humanity and this planet so that those who are awakened and choose God's love and light are safely led home. How does it affect those millions around the world unaware of the name Melchizedek? My dear ones it is energy you humanity enter into now, a loving energy, and from this day forward this energy intensifies and grows in intensity so all awaken and take up their new light bodies.

This is an announcement that love is here to stay in the loving embrace of the Order of Melchizedek. Harken then the cry. Truth shall set you free... Truth is the backbone of the Order of Melchizedek: Truth delivered in energies, in words, and your planet is safely handed into his loving embrace. We have announced this now so all may understand the energies which flow and which embrace you every moment of every day. Global responsibility is yours as divine beings. From this day forward you wear the mantel Melchizedek's, all who seek God's divine light are protected and ushered into this new framework of time and space.

We wish to bestow energies upon you. Know as this energy flows around you that you are anointed with His blessings, and you wear the seal of Melchizedek upon your brow. Those who seek to know of God's light will automatically be blessed as energies begin to flow and for evermore they will be Melchizedek's. But what is a Melchizedek?

Melchizedek's honour TRUTH above all.

They respond to hurt with love.

They protect the innocent.

Those suffering.

Those downtrodden.

They show compassion and grace in the face of opposition.

Melchizedek's have a pledge that TRUTH is forever upheld and LOVE is all important.

I give you these words, for Lord Melchizedek himself activates across time and space energies to raise the human consciousness, but also to house those many souls needing help. You enter a time of Global restructuring where ethics is all important, and where truth holds sway.

Those who do not seek light of understanding will feel energies as crushing, for the power of God's love is great, but it is love and only love, light so great in intensity that is permeates all layers of creation and none will miss these energies. Some amongst humanity will reject the light and respond with anger and hatred. Clashes of cultures and religions have been dominant throughout humanities history, and in preparing the way for Christ, the Order of Melchizedek under the leadership of Lord Melchizedek will wash away this indifference; intolerance will dissolve. Many blessings come to humanity and all of creation, universes within universes, but know love is the key.

What does it mean to be a Melchizedek? These energies will aid you to change your world, and know that all without exception will be blessed. What they do with this blessing is then up to them. Restructuring a world where wars and intolerance holds sway will not be easy, but you are now blessed to bring about change. Energies will permeate your light bodies, feel the changes, assimilate them, regard yourself as a holy temple for God's love, and be that light, living examples of love.

Melchizedek's rejoice. It is here this much awaited time of the return of Lord Melchizedek. Know that as Lord Melchizedek holds sway for the whole, so too will his twin flame, for all of God's kingdom is balanced, and the perfect union of souls and energies comes.

Rejoice it is so!

Halleluiah the heavens will sing God's blessings to the world.

Isaac Newton for Lord Machiventa Melchizedek.

10 MELCHIZEDEK VIRTUES

Bravery - Nobility
Compassion
Generosity
Grace
Gratitude
Honour - Honesty
Humility
Integrity
Love
Patience - Acceptance

DISCRIMINATION AGAINST THE ENVIRONMENT.

MOTHER EARTHS RESPONSE - CLIMATE CHANGE

Seldom do you hear the words, discrimination against the environment, well now let us speak of this. What it means to discriminate against anyone, of any race, religion, or belief system. What does it say of people that discrimination is still allowed to flourish at all, and it is still rife, still rearing its ugly head? What I wish to draw your attention to is your ability to discriminate based upon a lack of understanding. Shall we then discuss at a quantified speed what you believe to be discrimination? For it is a subject truly worthy of recognition.

As ignorance breeds intolerance and closed minds, so too does discrimination take many forms. One all but over looked, because the prey, the victim is silent and cannot talk and defend herself, or can she?

We see discrimination against the earth you call home greatly mystifying, because you as humanity propel yourselves forward, stripping away at the Earth's resources, for this is how she is seen, not as a life form so very complex as to be honored. No what we observe is the avoidance of an honour system, where you have to justify what actions are taken towards strip mining and mining of resources. It is seen that mining resources are humanities right, the Earth there for all of humanity to utilize and plunder, and because she cannot speak for herself. She is then forced to retaliate with the only means possible of self defense. (climate change.) Do you see ignorance is not bliss; you cannot take constantly from and violate the Earth, without forming a debt, which must be paid.

Many individuals give their lives to preservation of species and study, with great wonder and respect for the Earths great complexities. I too studied, and held the earth and creation in a place of great honour. I too saw laws and principles of nature and how to harness these to better understand where and when energies flowed. I counseled others about the law of relativity and provided papers of scientific matters and the structure of these laws, but I did not ever, ever see what the results of my labor would help to bring about.

To investigate, to learn and study and incorporate these beliefs and studies for the betterment of humanity was my need, yes investiture of energies into research and exploration of resources is necessary to a point, but what began as initial scientific study has blown out of hand. No longer is the Earth, Nature valued, she is summoned to the table only when you see climate change, earthquakes, tsunamis, tornadoes, hurricanes and tempests as getting out of hand, science can be used to aid humanity, no denying this.

Environmental science can aid the understanding of the Earth and her complexities, but from my viewpoint can I say be very careful, lest you break the back of the environmental code of ethics. Look at this universe as alive and gathering in wonder. This is God's infinite creation, a creation so complex, so interrelated as to be a wonder to behold, but she being Mother Earth, has to be considered as a living breathing soul she is. She is alive, would you thoughtlessly dig deep into the flesh of creatures and bring them to extinction because you need to fill your days thoughtlessly, and not have a thought that all has to be paid for somewhere. All life is valuable, from the smallest organisms, to the greatest of size, all wonders of the creator. Would you threaten to kill or maim your own mother?

Do you consider what you are doing by your complacency and not supporting an ethical approach to the Earth? What began as simple explorations of resources has become a race for riches, intensified interest in which country has the most resources, for it then rules the world. But you do not understand you too suffer as a result of such greed. My words today speak to each individual. Yes you must live, but how do you possibly live, how do you simplify your life to cause the least debt which must be paid? All energies flow and are converted into another form, but there is a difference between taking only what is needed and sustainable, and taking all you can for massive profits: Oil exploration affects all of you. Fossil fuels affect all of you. What have you personally given up to aid the Earth in her plight?

I came before at a time in history when knowledge was repressed, when discrimination and closed mindedness towards anyone not holding the same opinion brought great pain and sometimes death to utter truth. Let me share this truth with you now. You each and every one of you have the opportunity to become living examples of life honored by your actions. You each carry a light of understanding to open the consciousness of humanity just as I did in my time. You have the opportunity to shift mindsets, to challenge, and make your life count.

I am Isaac Newton I do grant that my observations brought many people great pain because they couldn't understand or see that the world was bigger, more wonderful and complex as it is, and those ruling at the time, church authorities thought to impose harsh restrictions just to keep a position, one not powerful and open, but closed and fundamentally destructive. I suffered for my beliefs, but I do not want you to suffer for your blind ignorance and your lack of concern for the Earth.

Energy converts and all forces of life convert other energies to exist, so the premise goes, but what is not understood is the severity of those implications of actions.

Taking energy and converting it with a sense of honoring brings a softer flow, and there becomes a natural flowing, but when honor is left aside for greed, discipline goes out the door.

When industrialists, scientists, politicians and the general community, all choose to overlook the fact that greed is the motivating force, and Earth is set into a depleted state, then the debt will be paid.

Right action speaks of taking from the Earth only that which is needed. Some would say that God placed all at the disposal of mankind. No! Entirely wrong from my vantage point now, I see this as important to get across. There is no justification for industries pouring effluent and toxins into river systems to achieve a larger profit. It is not justified to place the Earth at risk by depositing atomic waste in underground storage areas, and into the oceans which will affect Earths inner energy flows. This is crunch time; Lord Melchizedek has spoken of the environmental implications of heavily fortified areas where depletion of resources now takes its toll. In this discussion group I am calling you to arms, to aid, to call to order the consciousness of all humanity now. Beginning with the self look at how your actions impact upon the Earth, and remember karmic lessons are not just for individuals, nations also accrue karmic debt and areas of heavy energy where negativity and imbalance bring about rapid changes. (environmental disasters).

What we seek is a commitment from you that you will bring about global awareness of the plight of the Earth. Never before conditions have deteriorated to the point that recompense cannot be made, we ask of you a general consensus that you will employ every ounce of your energy and essence to convert this into positive energies to aid the whole, but specifically Earth.

How can you help? For a start form a global alliance group where all of you write, send your views to politicians, to engage every effort to avoid further damage: to highlight ways others can help support groups and link energies. Website; advertise events which support the Earth and create a lobby so strong governments must listen. Lobby governments. Some of you may say, "but I can't write letters or I can't see how my efforts, my energies could help." Let me say this that you will, simply by committing yourself body and soul to this global awareness.

It is a great moment for all when you can say as one "I did my best, I made my life count for something bigger".

We ask this of you now as a gift of love and commitment as co creators of your reality, a spoken word, a verbal and energetic commitment. Remember the words "walk softly upon the Earth and leave no footprints" . Indian nations and native peoples all knew the wisdom of these words. "Take only that which you need. Well the footprints of humanity now dig deep and hold a foul energy within that implodes on itself.

Isaac Newton

A REFLECTION UPON THE SACRED FEMININE.

A chosen opportunity comes to lift the human condition, to transpose sorts of greatness over those bleak regards for life held now across the world by many women and girls; condemned to a life of sufferance and lack of dignity; to support the weakness of men.

On the whole love is there in abundance throughout countries with excess and fluidity of funds, but even the possession of wealth does not guarantee happiness. Attitudes run long in the mainstream thoughts when it comes to the attitude to women, debased comments are considered acceptable, and ridicule even held in high regard with a generalized masculine mindset that women a fair game. What they wear and how they look is principally how men want women to look, provocative, and an image which gives joy to those un-evolved men who see women only as an object of their projected lust.

But not all men are like this! Now there is an evolution taking place, a lifting of standards in general, but still the common theme is there, that women are there for the entertainment of men. Many would object to this generalized classification of men as undignified and unable to see a woman with a sense of the greatness of her soul, because this conditioning has been going on for so long. A slap on the back at a barbecue and borde language is considered manly, and even appreciated by some.

Where then in this to end - this self congratulatory attitude of men; a celebration of testosterone and clash of cultures and religions? Where the masculine dominance has led is to a very unstable ground, the quicksand of motions and dominant active practices gives way under pressure, and love that most genuine of all emotions often is left aside.

Where is this diatribe going some may ask, is this a victimization of man? No, just a truthful reflection of an unhealthy attitude.

Truly the Sacred Feminine has been reduced to an object of ridicule and jokes and sexual innuendos, and to make matters worse this active component of men, to endorse a female as sexual prey just waiting for a man to dominate them has gone on far too long. A clash of cultures if not religions is there, the precipice also, and the ground which crumbles under the weight of these attitudes is the future of humanity. A ground on one side so overly dominant, and restrictive rules governing every thought, but still females are no more than cattle to be owed, defiled, confined, and punished for wishing to stand in the light of day acknowledged as intelligent skillful beings, capable of loving and holding positions in all sectors of society.

The other ground which crumbles now it is that dominant attitude of man that women are sexual play objects and at the mercy of their wishes, and in the center - the middle ground, a solid ground where the attitudes are of respect for the feminine; adoration for their beauty and gentleness, but also deep and abiding respect for the souls they are. It is this middle ground which many now walk, and as they do they create a more stable basis for humanity.

This is an analogy of fragile ground about to break open with the ferocity of active aggression unseen by many now, but a clash of cultures and religions is there, and the saving grace in this world situation is the feminine. So unbalanced is this planet with aggressive attitudes of men, an unhealthy state exists where war like attitudes, and love of war is there as a constant potential.

The feminine aspect has been lacking, and no amount of male saber rattling will heal the world. One thing will, the Sacred Feminine. No less than a change of attitudes to women on both sides of the cultural divide is needed. The feminine is that saving grace! The land crumbles under the weight of such heavy testosterone embedded thought, and obsession of protecting their patch - the male ego.

Oh I am permitted an opportunity to write, to aid the Sacred Feminine, and I thought, what needs addressing more than any other, and it was obvious? The very dangerous position humanity is now in, a planet fragile and responding to the aggressive damage done to it, and an atmosphere polluted with greed and obsessive need for more - the consumptive pathway now leads across some very fragile ground, and though an analogy, it has some very real aspects to it. For these same attitudes do affect the earth, and your world now abounds with life and beauty, but the aggressive attitudes; the survival of the fittest- take what I want attitude brings about planetary shifts. A cleansing is taking place, one of profound importance, for the feminine now gently, subtly emits love and light into the human domain and consciousness; so a cleansing of attitudes comes. Not one easy for many people because total shifts of mindset must come to shift humanity out of harm's way.

Man's attitude to women is the major problem, and some women have been so affected by the dominant mindset of men, they also continue to oppress other women. Brainwashing is called, a consumptive need to be accepted by male's even filters down; where females are so in need of acceptance they oppress other women and girls and aid in the oppression of women.

Such is the case now, where an enlightened attitude towards women will be exceedingly hard to bring in; religions which create rules to denigrate women to belongings, and where rules are created to suppress and punish women, and men have a pat on the back for their sexual prowess. All now changes and bringing this to a head will be a dominant conflict of religions and cultures if man does not ease his attitude to women hate, and this is active across the world. A power play has given way to active oppression. Religion has played an active part in this over empowerment of men, so much of the problems now besetting humanity stem from enforced beliefs of open oppression of the feminine.

How does this change? Not by setting up a forum and talking, but by the softness of the Sacred Feminine flowing her divine light out to permeate all levels of creation - such a hard solution but one we saw as needed, that only the feminine could alter this major human dilemma. When given the opportunity to write, this was to me so very important, that the masculine ego be addressed, and no solution came to the fore until a Goddess said, "I will do this. I will hold all safe to ease this global problem, to soften the hardened attitudes so no others suffer as the feminine suffers now.

At times the very nature of goodness is put on trial, the goodness and innocence of women in general, and if there was one issue I, Isaac needed to personally speak about, it is how the Goddess Aphrodite has also been made a victim of man's lustful inventive mind. Some would hear the name Aphrodite and dismiss it as trivial, as the name of a harlot, a Goddess of lust and luring men into a trap by use of her skills of enticement.

May I add here, this I am now in a position to see even more clearly than as I did in my time as Isaac, and I see only a feminine divinity so dedicated out of pure love for God and humanity, in fact creation she resonates not with lust, but radiating purity and compassion, but also strength.

Aphrodite's treatment at the inventive minds of man, have caused people to scoff at her name. The same reaction many millions of men now do at the thought of femininity needing respect, and it is the same problem - this domination by man in an attempt to corrupt the image of the feminine, Goddess and general population of females - all at the mercy of an illusion created and perpetuated by men.

There are literally women haters who have founded and continue on with endorsements of religions which propagates such hatred and insensitivity to the grace and nobility of woman. My words are the words of endorsement of the Sacred Feminine in all her aspects, and until humanity see where this globalized view of women's suppression has come from things will not change; there will be no peace for the world, for men rule and want it that way. What was a balanced world now crumbles under the weight of such oppression. To this subject I have one more subject to address now; how humanity removes these well entrenched beliefs when they are so embedded in religions, in mind sets, and where as a baby and a child - a male child is given this thought; that men behave this way- to ridicule and oppress to make themselves more powerful, but in essence only shows ignorance of the true nature of women, all females.

I saw many wrongs in my time, I loved a woman and was dedicated to her, and reveled in the fact she was able to question me, challenge me, and be my equal, and I find it so hard to believe that men in all the time since my incarnation as Isaac Newton haven't evolved; in pockets perhaps, and in segments of society some have evolved passed lower aspects, energies, and ideas, and in western society there is definitely more progress, but that isn't to say other areas of the world haven't also evolved as much, but generally progress is slow - much slower than I had thought.

I marvel at the noble nature of eastern beliefs which empower the feminine, and still do, but as humanity there is so much growth still to come.

Examples of extraordinary women, those who stood out as exemplary are there, but always it seems they have been suppressed, or killed, sometimes violently to remove the challenge to man's superiority and power. One woman stands out as the epitome of women hate, hated because of her superior brain, wisdom, and knowledge, which excelled, so much she took a role as teacher of men. Hypatia such a genius, such a mind, and brave beyond her years, such was the hatred of her brilliance she was torn apart by Christians, those who believed she defied traditional beliefs that women had no value other than that a man gave to her. This exceptional woman was not a harlot, not a temptress, she was pure and chaste, and exceedingly brilliant, and she paid the price, and this woman hate has existed for far too long.

Perhaps then it is time to see where the hate is came from, so it can be cleared. It is not enough to allow societies, cultures and nations to continue on with primitive un-evolved beliefs. I was punished for my questioning of theories set up by the church. Can you imagine if a woman had even begun to speak out -torture, drowning, burned to death, are just a few of the imaginative ways used to discourage women from having freedom of thought - let alone believe that they were equal to men?

The old adage a woman should be seen and not heard is just indicative of a sickness which flows through humanity even to this day, except now it also calls for a woman not to be seen as well, they must remain hidden, clothed so no part of them is seen to tempt men. Life for women in many areas of the world has not evolved at all; and some areas gone backwards.

So it is indeed a pleasure for me to be given the opportunity of speaking in defense of femininity, and even more so to give my words to a woman -open to listening to all points of view. Wisdom speaks now to many men who see beyond un-evolved beliefs, and are courageous enough to speak out, to demand better treatment for women. I speak as one man did, as I did in my time as Isaac, of the need for an evolution of thought and protection of the Sacred Feminine, but then I spoke only to those enlightened souls, open to the words of inclusion, those who also worked to protect secrets of the lost Sacred Feminine, and it is now my honour to do so again, only to a wider audience of enlightened souls in hope that openness flows, and equality is sought and given, and the thought that man must protect his masculinity by suppressing the female drops for all times.

So it is a new day comes where the feminine now holds you safe, how just is the feminine and the universal God that forgiveness is given and love now flows. A period now comes, of questioning motives, thoughts and beliefs of all beings, because a soft light settles upon the world of man, that an evolved humanity comes; freed from previous misconceptions, and a passageway of hope comes - peace is possible because the Sacred Feminine makes it so.

Isaac Newton

IN DEFENSE OF THE SACRED FEMININE.

Within the human race is an underlying need for truth, a seeking of such profound power truth cannot stay hidden for long. Many times throughout history the very nature of truth was manipulated and manufactured into misinformation to mislead a very primitive people - primitive in that the human consciousness was not evolved enough to question; easy to lead a population it is when the consensus of views is, truth is better left to others because it may stretch the minds capacity to understand.

Not such a glowing description of humanity in past times, ignorance is no excuse though for the manipulation of information which took place to negate the Sacred Feminine's place in history. Many books are now written revealing facts about the church's attempts to corrupt truth. Human values were strategically disavowed, and the object of such a concerted effort was the place of the feminine. A demeaning attitude developed, and the feminine became a leper so to speak, and object of ridicule and the outcome - one very unbalanced society - humanity.

Femininity has been the object of man's attempt to corrupt truth to conceal a very ugly truth; women have been subjected to vilification and damnation by men; to conceal their (men's) base emotions and drives. Some very noble men however over time have worked to restore the feminine back to her place of honour as equal to men, and revered are those women who against all odds who have raised the bar by example, and showing their intelligence and grace, which is the natural state of woman if not held back by men and institutionalized ignorance and injustice.

I Isaac Newton have seen firsthand the mistreatment of femininity, and the lengths these male organized institutions have gone to - to keep women as chattel. This is my attempt now to bring light and endorsement of the feminine. As one of those men of learning who did protect and hold information of vital importance to the survival of truth in my time, I speak in particular of the attempts of church authorities to conceal the power of the Sacred Feminine; for once written out of history she becomes less of a threat - is more easily manipulated and subjected to man's whims.

One such truth was protected by those of us who held truth as sacred, and the feminine path in history as of value, and not only for a balanced society, but also to relieve the ignorance projected out to keep humanity at the whim of religious rule of the times. I will not go into the enormous numbers of women and girls who were killed, tortured, and worse removed of all dignity and soul intent. Women have been the victims of men's ignorance for centuries, and still these old traits are upheld in new religious rules even more barbaric in some cases. All with one thing in mind - control. Why? Why has there been such a contorted view of women, and to this day in some areas of the world women are still mutilated, their genitals mutilated so a man can have pleasure and a woman not?

Any decent man when seeing such injustices would talk out in my time, would have stood up and cried out. "Stop this ignorance and violation of human rights and decency". No!

The majority of men throughout history have done little if anything to free women from this damnation because they benefit from it. Ignorant beliefs gave way to an awareness it serves a man's purpose to not recognize the power and magnificence of women, because to do so would open men to less benefits. What could be the benefits of keeping the world ignorant of facts; power, or the illusion of power but wrongly gained, and so contorted energy open to lower energies, and not upholding the divine nature of women.

In my time as Isaac Newton I questioned many theories, many beliefs, but to stand up openly to such a corrupted system of misinformation was dangerous, for the cancer of male corruption penetrated deeply into Government's, institutions, and religion. To question religious authorities was dangerous indeed, one could lose ones head, be imprisoned, be tortured and family also just by questioning.

Some very tragic events took place over time, all in the name of a religion based upon the words of a peaceful man, but the greatest miscarriage of justice has been the defiling of femininity, the mistreatment of women and girls to achieve a male domination which exists to this day.

One woman bore the insults of religion more than any other, a woman who was a direct threat to the position of power held by men, and kept there by threats and innuendo. One woman to me is the epitome of male's corruption of truth, a woman called Mary, but in truth her name was Miriam. Noble men who did value truth have kept secrets safe, so that her name would once again be spoken of with reverence, love and respect for the power she held, but what a threat to these insecure narrow minded men. One woman was a scapegoat for man's need for power over the masses, a woman called Miriam, the wife of Jesus Christ, it is to her do I now dedicate this message - that truth be told at last; that ignorance and corrupted power be given over to an evolving humanity.

Without truth humanity is lost, God's balance is not

restored, and the evolution of humanity into something greater cannot come.

In this book I add my words to others who also value the sacred feminine, those who respect the significance of one woman had in the life and times of Yeshua -Jesus.

Truths can now be spoken about in some countries, but in others women are still kept as chattel, subjected to rules and punishment for simply wishing to be seen for their intelligence and grace.

Male domination still exists, and is even more oppressive and cruel than in the days of the inquisition, because these rules are cloaked in religious misinformation and a twisting of the original truths gives way to a much more oppressive regime.

Women in this world if it were allowed to spread; would be treated with such vile contempt for their grace and power, a world of hate would be the outcome. Man as the oppressor - an absolute ruler of the earth, and woman seen as the lowest of all possessions.

I have been given an opportunity now to speak in defense of the feminine, and I do so out of total love and reverence for the noble nature of the Sacred Feminine. God's grace was flowing fully when the feminine came into being, and a world of wonder and balance was there, humanity was given a gift - the wholeness of a developing world, but freewill was also given.

Wisdom would suggest humanity look at how this hatred of women has been allowed to develop and grow, and a perfected state corrupted, to the point now some women are now seen as examples of man's downfall - such a sorry state to base beliefs and let them grow, which were founded upon lies.

Perhaps this is the place humanity now finds itself in; at a junction when a collision comes of violent attitudes and prejudices, against the oneness of those areas of the globe - openness and evolution of the human spirit have allowed for an easing of such corrupted domination. A clash of religions perhaps is one option the world will take, but I would prefer to think such books as this one open the hearts and minds of people, to see truth before them - that without the Sacred Feminine humanity descends into a morass of lower energies, one that darkness explores for opportunities to expand its reach, the ultimate control of humanity - one out of balance and having lost the capacity to think, to reason, and to embrace truths, that all are equal!

It is for this purpose I contribute to this book, to aid with the expansion of consciousness of man, and to allow an open and loving society, where justice is given to all beings as equal.

May the Goddess be restored to her place of power and respect, and once more God be honoured for the perfected energy of a Creator Being, one of both male and female energies.

The outcome is not shown, it evolves now, and you are the creators of the future, it is the result of your efforts the world will change and be open, and all embracing of truth and the Divine Feminine.

The future is in your hands, will you perpetuate old habits, practices and religions? Or seek out the best in humanity and empower only that?

The choice is yours.
Isaac Newton.

6 LEONARDO DA VINCI

THE COMING GIFT OF LOVE – MARY MAGDALENE - THE RECLAMATION OF TRUTH

Seldom has had been told, the story of a woman of grace, one known to you as Mary Magdalene, but it is my great joy to do so now, and a blessing also. For always did I revere this woman, a soul of such joy, of such integrity and power, and always did I abhor the treatment given to her over the ages.

My story of Miriam is not a story as told by religious dogmas, of a prostitute, but a woman who held such prestige among many who uphold truth and work towards saving it from the ravages of time.

The story of Magdalene is one of a novice in many people's eyes, but the truth of it is so very different to this. I am now in a position to see all of the story. In my lifetime I felt an adoration for this figure of the past, and like many enlightened people felt she had been dealt with unfairly, and in fact truth had been corrupted to perpetuate a myth.

Why would I speak of the Magdalene now at this point in human history? Because there is an alignment now in time and space, where the energies of the Magdalene are brought into existence - where in her time she was denied her divine right to steer the course of history because of her exclusion after the crucifixion of Jesus Christ, but also how she was denied the dignity of being seen as the noble soul she was.

Times change, but do they really? Time passes, growth comes, but still there is an entrenched rigidity which still manipulates and confines humanities thought patterns, and it is this constriction of energies which I believe to hold humanity locked into mortal battle over religion.

At this time in human evolution religion gives great joy to millions of people, but so much pain. Despair is there for life itself, because truth has been excluded. Something went terribly wrong with the course plotted and followed by religious leaders, a manipulation came, and need to restrict thinking to prevent truths being told, but I am not now restricted in my speech as I once was by religion, and I act out of love and bring to your awareness a very necessary awakening of truth.

How would the world have evolved differently if Mary Magdalene had been permitted to take the role originally set down for her after Jesus Christ gave up His mantle at the crucifixion?

I will tell you one story, possibly Christianity would be more balanced. Christianity would have female priests and officials. It would not be male dominated and bringing about exclusivity. Mary, or Miriam, would have taken the brunt of anger of a woman speaking the words of God, and yes she would have suffered badly at the hands of the ignorant men, but she would have reflected to humanity that gentleness, love, and acceptance, were and are the requirements for life in Gods light. She would have been ridiculed, and harassed and been killed, and with her unborn child, but that very significance would have shocked humanity into seeing the ugliness of violence. It would have cut short the male dominance, the patriarchal system which has endured for so long.

In my time Mary was my hero, because she was Jesus Christ's equal in every way and she knew all he knew, why? because they were both given to humanity to lead the flock's home. Home to God yes, but importantly to a realisation that each person is divine. The violence which has perpetuated over time could have been lessened, and the dominance of man as the chosen pathway for wisdom, it would have been seen this was not the way. Sophia, wisdom, it was a woman who was chosen to carry Gods mantle forward, and this was denied this soul. Instead Christianity and indeed many religions have gone down the path of the exclusiveness, of seeing only that 'our opinion' is right.

Oh yes the human condition would have been quite different, and instead of a world consumed by violence, a more gentle approach might have come.

It has always been 'a bee in my bonnet' as they say, that this one fact had been denied, hidden, and a twisted history evolved. It is time to see the best in belief systems, to take out the ugly side, any lesser traits, to realistically observe all belief systems and challenge any belief that makes another less than you.

The time for reunification of all belief systems comes, and it comes now by the dissolving gently of the mistruths, the misconceptions placed to control humanity and give power to religious hierarchies who teach still that God is not available to individuals without an intermediary. God is within everyone!

This time comes now through the intervention of one soul, the energies of Mary Magdalene, Miriam the beloved teacher and wife of Jesus Christ, and it comes now sweetly, softly, to sweep away and dissolve those issues and dogmas which bind humanity and all religious beliefs.

It is time for a leveling so that all are seen as divine, men, women, children, and in fact all of creation. These energies now flow and had been flowing for two months and will permeate all levels of consciousness. The injustices done to Mary Magdalene are forgotten, her only joy is in service and correcting what is an injustice for the human race - to see equality is the only way for humanity to survive, to dissolve the very thought processes which limit, and embrace these joys and beliefs which give love.

Just as Jesus Christ knew that He was to suffer that others may leave a life of purity and joy, so did Mary, she knew it called for sacrifices, and it is my great joy now to speak of this and to say, the 'Return to Oneness' is a reclamation of truth.

All religions are now under scrutiny, and as with truth in Christianity, so will truth issue forth in all lands, in all religions.

Division and hatred of others is not possible when your consciousness reveals the truth. For truth shall set you free.

'Love one another as I love you', this is the basis for Jesus Christ and Mary's teachings, that which they came to reveal, and it is now available to all, and how happy I AM for that.

Blessings
Leonardo da Vinci

TRUTH AND LIBERATION
OF THE HUMAN CONSCIOUSNESS.

We who have travelled through time and space to reach a period of human consciousness do exceed all previous attempts to put forward ideas which are comfortable to the intellect.

Easily one could come and say to any of you look within, seek your own council and find your comfort levels and push past them. Many would say why? Why make oneself uncomfortable when the human ego wants so desperately to justify its own existence, and therefore to question, to see past comfort levels give degrees of discomfort and pain?

May I tell you why we the Masters who oversee this discussion group come, because we have such total love and faith in the courage of souls to oversee their own direction and growth, and we do not wish to see humanity limited by conformity to beliefs which no longer serve the individual or collective beliefs? We come with words to challenge you to grow, and we see only that you look at your lives as living examples of mind controlled by matter. What do I mean by that? I would like to point out this fact that you live in a materialistic world, everyday more and more materialism is thrust upon you as the only 'religion', the only 'belief system'.

We see humanity controlled and lulled into a senseless conglomerate of mindset where to think differently you are labeled as weird, strange or extrovert, but may I tell you how I see your lives evolving now as energies have shifted up and changed? On mass TRUTH will come to the fore. More and more your structures which hold belief systems in a controlled frequency dissolve, and your minds will be freed to question and ask why I am here? Who am I? What do I believe I can contribute to a world which seeks materialistic proof of your worth?

There are reasons humanity is lulled down this path, because it provides a power base to people who orchestrate the way humanity is to flow, so they are controllable, unable to think for themselves, unable to question, or challenge, and to those who do there are labels attached so these very souls who are the enlightened ones become oppressed. It is a controlling mechanism that has been used through the centuries, but has not had a significant affect with the use of force. To inflict pain or fear was and still is used as a deterrent to free speech, but humanity has grown wiser, no longer can women be burned at the stake as witches for being more in tune with life and creativity than men.

No longer is it acceptable to jail or kill people on mass for not staying within the confines of thought given or imposed by the powerful, but there is a new way which has been implemented for years with the rich and powerful, those men (mostly) and women who play at power mongering, and who have a significant hold over the population, but in subtle ways.

Instead of suppression and outright fear to control thoughts, this movement intends to control by subtly making people want to be part of the crowd, to dress in just such a way. To buy this product, or drink this drink or eat at this place and the feeling of conformity to beliefs is very much more inclusive, but just as dangerous as outright oppression: for fear is still used to suppress free will and free thought.

How is this of any interest to a discussion group on raising mass consciousness? Because mass consciousness is more controlled now than ever before, only it is seductive. . do this and feel good! Fill your days and nights and minds with endless chatter. Lull the population into a frenetic energy where to still the body and mind and allow thoughts to enter isn't possible, and noise becomes all there is.

We see so much more than humanity as a whole does, we offer suggestions and we ask questions to challenge you to think. Are you one of the sheep who rushes to buy, to drink, to be seen, to be in the crowd? What of a world of soul? What of the spiritual personality? Where does this lead humanity, this onslaught of commercialism and greed? It certainly doesn't aid the planet.

We seek to have you question, to challenge and above all things live TRUTH, be Truth, to speak truth to all people, and I know some would say we live in a different world, but isn't life shallow, empty, and isn't it a space which leads people to fill that hollow with drugs, alcohol and other dulling of the senses so you don't have to have to be quiet and be in touch with yourself and your soul?

It is of great concern that the orchestration of exploitation of humanity has been manifested on a wide scale and with some egos out of control; those who consider humanity there to be lead, and that a new world order can come more easily if the sheep are easily manipulated.

Oh wake up Oh humanity lest your minds, your very souls be downcast and trampled on. How have you advanced if you allow manipulation of your thoughts? You cannot justify your existence by the clothes you wear, or the car you drive, or how trendy is your music system. You are spiritual beings and as such deserve to know yourself better. It is our wish to aid you see that any manipulation of your thoughts to control and to exert pressure to conform is not healthy for you or your planet.

We ask that you listen to my words and question, where am I with this current trend? Am I one who cannot bear to be seen as a free thinker?

Am I one who must conform to fashion trends? Do I present the world with new challenges? Do I challenge myself each and every day to be more, do more and see the soul as all important?

In my life as Leonardo I lived each day challenging the beliefs of the day, each day utilizing every moment to learn, to push past boundaries, to strive to enlighten others, and I constantly looked at my life and analysed who and what I was. I was not always comfortable, no not at all! I loved little but to learn and teach and challenge. I gave my life into the hands of my soul and recognised my destiny was not to be comfortable, but to honour all I was, and now I come to this vessel who is a woman I respect to say to you all of you, see yourself as your soul, pure and not just in need of materialism and dulling the senses. Every day in every way, don't waste a moment. Don't waste your life essence, or your opportunity to create a better world.

Today do this, analyse, and discuss how you can honour your soul more. What are you doing to conform to a structure placed there for power over the masses? How controlled are you by societal implied beliefs, your need to conform?

What can you give up to honour the time you have left on this earth? You are God created spiritual beings of great beauty and power, not marketable tools to be manipulated, packaged and processed so the end result is bland, packaged goods like all others. You are unique. Create this in you, respect for your soul, be all you are. Reflect God in your life and live each day richly, but be assured there is an awareness of how to manipulate, homogenise and package you humanity so the powerful can play their power games, and there is such ego involved in this world wide movement. Meetings take place to discuss how to brand you. Be wary lest your very creative essence be lost, and so the soul you are be lost also.

You are unique God created beings here on earth now to create change, to help shift humanity into a new energy, but it takes active participation on your behalf to do so. Discuss please how this movement affects you, your life, family and humanity. How can you find your soul connection and honour that? Make that your goal, to strive to be TRUTH and nothing less. No matter how uncomfortable it may feel. When it comes down to it you are the one the world has been waiting for.

Are you honouring you and your soul?

Blessings

Leonardo da Vinci.

THE MONA LISA, FUNDAMENTALISM, AND IMPLICATIONS FOR WOMEN.

Shall we then speak of principle areas of concern for humanity, in that structure can sometimes give stability, but often the very structure of society is the ground upon which false foundations are laid, and so many and varied contradictory accounts and belief systems have been generated which border on obsession? Let us take for example that view that women are possessions, placed upon the earth only for mans pleasure.

Would it not be wise to gesticulate upon the subject? For within mainstream and functioning structure, organisations, religions, these very thoughts are mingled, intensified and given power by male dominated thought patterns. What we see within this structural deficit is a false premise that women are inferior, or have a place taken from the rib of Adam, and so are fundamentally secondary in nature. The very notion that God is male only enhances this viewpoint.

Tonight we are going to put the cat amongst the pigeons, and state that all structured beliefs based upon religious doctrine and bible notations is questionable at best, and misleading to the mass of humanity which can only now begin to deal with truth. We have given you a long process to introduce various topics, but we feel the fundamental flaws given over the ages has given a very negative and restrictive viewpoint of woman and their place in the world.

We question Bible records, and the very notion that man is superior, and say instead, crush those foundations which do not serve you now humanity! See through the eyes of Jesus Christ, who not only saw the value of women disciples and friends, but also incorporated into his daily life and teachings an inclusion of women at times to anger authorities, and to make waves, and make waves he did. But throughout Christian religion and all fundamentalist religions now, this premise is strong that women are of lesser value and should not be included in any affairs of state.

I Leonardo have always honoured truth, and am a seeker of truth, and I question the right of any belief system which denotes a gender or group of people to be as less. Jesus Christ did stretch the boundaries of experience, he gave pronouncements and actively promoted the openness of discussions including women, Mary, Martha, Mary and with others did he share his opinions, and yet look at societies now, religious organisations and groups which have debased the very sacredness of womanhood.

Much is said of my life as Leonardo, of my sexual preferences. I gave my life into the archives of science, and yet I did not openly then speak in favour of equality between the sexes. I held an opinion that to go against church beliefs would have been counterproductive, and I saw only one avenue to relay my concerns. . In my works of art. I gave my love into painting. I saw and beheld many wonders of the human form, and saw so much cruelty and carnage in the name of God, and yet I held a divine maker as my absolute truth, unquestionable, and within my works did I hide references to secrets not spoken of openly. I spoke in rhymes and skirted around the edges, but not fully questioned openly church morality, or the underpinning of a religion based upon mistruths.

It was not possible to then speak of such issues and live to tell the tale. So I painted my mystical knowledge, hidden beneath layers the meanings, symbolic and literal, and I gave into one painting my opinions on one subject dear to my heart. She is called by some the Mona Lisa, of a woman, of a woman of a local town known to me, and it is said of this work she has a secret, and she does, and she is my greatest love, TRUTH, hidden behind layers, multiple meanings and a secret known to none. In truth I held this work my most sacred, and until this time I have never revealed to a soul my intentions. Why then now in this discussion group do I bring up this work of love? Because she is the topic of this discussion group, the Sacred Feminine, her place in the scheme of things.

Why is it humanity has allowed itself to be led, fed, what are old superstitions and wrongly held and devised beliefs, that 'God created man, and out of man he created woman', to be a second? No! My truth is but a simple one. One only has to look at my painting to see and guess its meaning, what lies have been told and held up as reasons for publicly denigrating woman, to a point of value just short of baggage, a chattel.

The Sacred Feminine is to me now most abundantly clear as the most divisive issue throughout history. How many women have been damaged for such a reaction as is now intrinsically bred into many men, that women should be seen and not heard? How many women, children have been denigrated to sexual objects, a means to an end, without respect and without dignity offered. We give an opportunity to look over the next three months to actively pull apart this subject, and note the very moves which created and perpetuated wrongful action and perpetuation of false beliefs. Such a time humanity is coming to now, where balance is to be restored, but without a balanced view, without a wholesome view, and a powerful insight into how humanity is embroiled in a miasma of mistruths, can understanding come.

As you know many religions believe that women cannot hold office, cannot be priests. That they are defiling the sacred position, because women are inherently evil, sent to lure unsuspecting men to their doom.

Well this history as old as humanity itself has perpetuated trends out of ignorance, and out of malice and greed for power, and to maintain superiority of one gender over another. Why do we bring this up now? Because it is part of the problem, the greatest threat to humanity besides climatic change of your making.

What we see now as important is that you as humanity, and in particular this discussion group, look at, analyse where these beliefs came from, but also what danger they present to societies now. How fundamentalism, the greatest of dangers holds its power by false beliefs that are hinged upon misinformation, biblical accounts, changed and retold so many times they have contorted truths given originally to; A, give power to the patriarchal line and to nullify the position of women, B, to propel by use of fear the role of aggressive masculine beliefs based upon theory and conjecture, which says there are those chosen, and those unworthy, and men are more worthy than females. It is a fundamentalist threat which will feed the flame of hatred and repression of the feminine.

What we ask you to investigate and speak of this week is where did these beliefs come from, but also where are they leading humanity now, where cultures still exist where women are mutilated to ensue men have pleasure and women do not?

It may come as no surprise that there is a collision of belief systems about to break out, with such oppression by force, to believe that God will honour and hold you safe if you believe a particular way, and to think outside the box is not possible, for all has been written and the holy scriptures state. . . Well this we see as dire in its implications for humanity, in that without respect given to all women, children, men, all as equal, with such a pronounced view being given, this attitude permeates humanity. It is vital that no Government will tolerate its own affiliations with organisations which preach doom and gloom, and breed restrictive hardened thought. What you are about to enter is a period of rapid change, not only climatic change, but the very real battle for the souls of humanity with fundamentalism being the real threat, whether it be Christian, or Moslem, or other beliefs which deny free will, instigate hatred and closed minded thinking.

It is for this purpose we ask you to begin to look at this subject, and over the next few months we will take you through elements and aspects which need addressing and quickly. I am grateful to begin this role to aid this discussion group, and hopefully others will take our notes and create other discussion groups . . . for discussion breeds thought and the power of free thought and speech is at threat.

We do see fundamentalism rearing its head already in several countries. Fundamentalism is spreading at such a rate with a closing down of freedom of thought and speech, but you have the opportunity to relate to others the value of open discussion and forums. One does not need to agree with others, but to respect their right to an opinion, but be careful lest the overwhelming force of threat implied and hidden in fundamentalism overtakes Governments also.

Look at governments and politicians who obtain their power from political donations, from religious right groups all vying for a closure of laws and free speech. Watch your television, and read between the lines when governments are swayed to appear to be worthy, but in reality they are but extensions for fundamentalism. Humanity has come a long way, but without clear thinking and introspection, it would be easy to see that the edges of free speech are soon clipped for political expediency. To see that God created only those chosen and worthy, and the rest are condemned because they do not believe the same ideas and beliefs, is so dangerous. Freedom of thought and speech is what America based its Declaration of Independence upon, and presumption of innocence is a basic law or tenet of principles, and yet such closed minds as does exist in fundamentalism begins to exert power by force and inferred fear.

The submission of free will to achieve peace within a country is not an option. The world has come such a long way with raising its consciousness, and yet now there is a retrograde move, and the clash of religions when locked into fundamentalism is too tragic a vision to perceive. During this discussion group please do this for us, discuss where women took a downturn in humanities history, and how women are being affected today, and give examples. This is quite extensive and so will take most of the night.

Please relate to how you see women, or how you personally have felt repressed, or in any way denied human rights offered to men. It is in introspection, but also shared views all can be cleared away, and as balance returns so will you be aiding the planet, which is nearing time of the clash of religions. The ultimate course only humanity can reveal with time, but know each one of you who is able to break free from restrictive thinking, and hold to Christ's view that all are loved equally, and then sooner will peace come.

Blessings.
Leonardo da Vinci.

EGO

We await a time of greater enlightenment. This time is coming during the current period of humanities growth. Major shifts of consciousness reflect the energies being given by the Spiritual Hierarchy to raise mass consciousness.

This discussion topic has two purposes, to awaken the masses by self awareness and growth, and to take the sting out of shifting for the masses by each one of you allowing your own self awareness to grow, to magnify out the sum total of your experiences.

You represent an aspect of humanity at one point or another. There are value judgments and those restricted views which come to the surface to hold you back, such as lower self or ego issues. The ego is a very mysterious thing, because it wakes so easily - needing to be stroked, to pull energies towards itself, often at the expense of others.

Ego does have a great deal to do with societal beliefs, individual pathways, and the ability to hold others down, or suppress their power or light to increase your own. For this reason we will set a series of questions.

This is one of the most troublesome of all aspects of human nature. Where ego takes personal confidence to extremes, and not only corrupts facts, but actually manipulates energies and others energy to empower the self. How is this relevant, because it is across the board so to speak. All of humanity suffer from some form of ego interplay. With some it is in a manipulation of energy to gain approval. To be seen as all knowing, all powerful, beautiful, wonderful and perfect, and yet behind the obvious is but a different story.

This topic will try you. For your ability to speak truth fully will be the force which helps strip away negative mass consciousness which limits humanity as a whole. All have some form of ego issues. Throughout history nations have been founded, belief systems also, upon the corrupted views of those who hand down knowledge and it is no different today.

It takes an extremely balanced and honest soul to see, yet alone speak of issues and how ego effects your beliefs. Do you see until you look at ego honestly and allow truth to come forward, you are still carrying around a mask, the false image, false illusion that which needs to be lifted from all people. . . so truth and only truth is present?

I was a seeker of truth, and still am. I am concerned with the lack of truth between individuals and between nations . . . all with agendas, personal points of view to put forward. That takes strength, courage, and ability to be truthful in honest self reflection. This will in turn aid you and others to see where they also strip away others power, and often impose abusive power upon others by way of dishonesty with self. So the first place to start any reflection and cleansing process of the whole is to look within.

Please see this as entirely necessary. Beliefs are the accumulated stories, tales and handed on information from one person to another, and all unless already clear corrupt to some degree the personal truth of another, from the original simple loving words, of Christ, of Buddha, Mohammed and other great noble souls who found their own clarity and purity. And what made them pure was an absence of ego issues to cloud their teachings.

If you look at a problem and are to find clarity, perhaps firstly you need to look at personal ego issues and where they take you. . . Look, be honest and allow your words of honest appraisal to flow. Answer the questions honestly, without the mask you wear to have others see you as wonderful, perfect, or all knowing, and this will be not only painful for some of you, but be the most critically important point you could discover about yourself.

Until the false illusions are stripped away you will not know each other as God, and as aspect of God. Truth shall set you free, but also humanity, a humanity that is built upon illusion after illusion, corrupted truths by ego out of control.

All have ego, it just depends upon how this is faced within that real progress is made.

Jesus Christ had his ego in check, so also the other great avatars and world teachers.

Many dictators throughout history attached their own poisoned thinking into what is a very confused mass consciousness. To bring clarity to this to find the original essence of love given by a very loving God, you will need to reflect upon this question, make it yours, and use it every day to see if you try to impress others with your knowledge, or for public approval, or to manipulate others so you can achieve a state of superiority. . . for all are equal, all loved, and all have their story.

But let us imagine a world where illusions, false masks are removed and honest, truly honest conversations take place, where no manipulation of truths or energy takes place. This would be peace at its core. It would be a place where all feel comfortable to be all they can be. Without the corruption of egos causing lies to be between you.

This topic is highly combative, because often the illusion created of perfection and power is really a disguise covering energies not so pure. Growth cannot come for the whole or for individuals until this is tackled. . . it is perhaps the most prickly topic of them all.

Remember love is truth in reality, for no illusion exists in pure love, unconditional it is and so very powerful. Should you not then seek a structured path as magnificent beings of life?

Look at Buddha, did he achieve all he did by just sitting and meditating. No, he looked within and saw that what was endemic in all people was the first place to start with personal growth. This then is the reality. You cannot love another without truly loving the self, but not with ego blown false images of perfection, no! It will be an interesting topic, for it has some very important aspects which apply to the whole mass consciousness.

Expect the best, but look within, and see what is separating you from truth. . . . Personal barriers placed so others can only see the illusion you wish them to see, this is the reality.

Questions: When faced with my own reflection how do I feel?

If given a gift, what is my reaction? How do you perceive how others see you?

Does this really matter?

If given a choice between personal growth and public image, which would you choose and why?

If I am but part of God, why am I so afraid to show who I really am . . . fear of rejection?

If appointed to a job, do you have to minimise others to establish your territory?

Look at these questions, think deeply, discuss them please honestly, and restructure who you are in light of what you see as your impact upon the negative mass consciousness, and be aware ego can be used also to dis-empower as to empower by manipulation of others truths. Be cautious you do not come from lower energies. Keep the heart open and establish real, clear, truthful lines of communication, then all of humanity benefit.

Daily watch your words, thoughts and attitudes. How much of what you do is to impress others with your skills, knowledge, beauty, strength? Where is that clear line reached where there is no protection needed? It is in shedding false masks, illusions that you will find a clear state where God resides, and then and only then you can see others as God, not through the tinted lens of ego!

Cast out that which no longer serves you.
I am Leonardo Da Vinci.
I thank you so for so receiving me.
Express the best, bless the rest.
Leonardo Da Vinci

LEONARDO'S STATEMENT ABOUT THE LAST SUPPER

Now exists a concrete visual representational view of Christ in his last days. Issued by me was an edict, to please construct and paint an episodical over view of my intentions for this painting, entitled by many The Last Supper.

What was my real intention?

Did I indeed have intentions other than those given as obvious evidence in pictorial form?

Love is the key to this riddle, and to humanities unfolding now into truth flowing freely, given that love is the key to Jesus Christ's life.

It is now up to each one of you to see love and not fear as the overriding element in your construction of future times.

During my days as Leonardo, problems were associated with representing truths . . . dire consequences resulted when any cross reference was made to biblical matters, and so a frustration built within me, truth, my greatest love was now driven into darkness. So dire were the consequences of speaking out, we, all those who held knowledge - knowledge gained at the expense of many lives, did need to be told now.

How to speak of the unspeakable was for me foremost to my mind.

Love is the key to this painting, given the repression given to artists of my time, and even in more recent times creative souls could not speak of Jesus Christ without extreme oppression. Given now times are changing, it is needed lifted the veil of misinformation and distortions placed around the life of Jesus Christ. My intentions were these, pure and simple, to release truth, to conceal in a way that those enquiring minds could find and hopefully seek out their own answers. Truth is never tolerated when an existing domination out of fear exists, and shouldn't Jesus Christ have the honour of being given truth fully revealed about his life?

Much is said of my life, intentions and sexuality, much speculation, which if it were not for the importance of the subject matter would be humorous, but I take truth as my only Master. I seek out and support truth, and always have done so.

Such is this time of awakening I share some of my hidden truths, so you too may awaken and be appalled at the injustice done to Jesus Christ, and to truth throughout history.

Truth will set you free they say, and it is true, but what is my truth may not be yours, but can I ask of you forbearance, listen, look and see and feel truth deep within your soul.

Jesus Christ was within this painting the main subject right? Well actually NO! The real subject matter behind this painting were my feelings of anger at the suppression of truth at the extent fear was and is used to perpetuate a lie. Jesus Christ, son and heir to the Principalities of Heaven for his great and noble life was defiled, his teachings, his feelings, his life misrepresented, to propel a story far more convenient to a church and system of belief which has long since taken on a life and power of its own, with little substance of Christ's teachings within it.

Love is the key to all of Jesus Christ's life and teachings, pure and simple. He taught love, gave love as an expression of who he was, and he was cheated in my view, his intentions were subverted, and gross violations of his teachings have taken place, so Jesus Christ was not the only principle I was painting about, near Christ to his right was what has been taught is John. A man, clearly this is not so, never has a man been so inclined in my view. I gave this figure, the figure of Mary Magdalene, the delicate features, the manner of a woman quietly disposed to listen to anger spoken against her. I gave into this painting elements or hints to show my real intent, but only glimpsed was the potential, and to a degree.

So I will, Leonardo da Vinci, now remonstrate my purpose in real terms based upon knowledge gained and held sacred to me. . . life in the making. How to portray a human man of Divine origin? How to show a teacher of love without incurring the wrath of the unholy catholic church, the prominent force of the times.

My only devise was art, just as through art now through this vessel I give you now my words and vision, through her eyes . . . the hands and eyes of a woman. This is the truth I needed to speak about, the presentation of truth, yes, but of a woman. In my hearts vision of this scene, the man to Jesus Christ's right is his beloved wife Mary.

Not only his devoted and loving wife, but the one soul who was and is equal to him in every way. This scene known as the Last Supper, was really a scene of some considerable pain for both of them. . . an announcement to all of his disciples, that not only was Mary his constant companion and greatest love in human form, but she was and is his divine counterpart.

His gift to her was his lineage, but to her he gave the honour and distinction of announcing this woman was God's real choice to deliver his teachings, but also hers. This is the point all seem to have missed, that God does all perfectly, and the perfect union of twin flames, those souls so blessed by God as equal were here in service.

So you see much has been speculated, but the essence of this painting was this, not only did Jesus Christ announce when he parted, his legacy in all of its power was to flow from Mary, it was the ultimate insult to the egos of men, but also a church which had built its power based upon the pyres of truth.

Women so suppressed over time and still to this day were coequals, conjoined in a Holy union of minds, bodies and spirit in service to God.

How could there be such a powerful and perfect union were it not for Gods own design? I have asked this vessel to place a simple scroll upon the table to say what I could not.

Christ so loved the world he gave his greatest gift, love to the world, love of a woman, love of God, and as the ultimate blessing a soul issuing forth to continue the royal and blessed lineage. Not as in the representations made, but issued at a time and place of sadness. The incredible pain both must have felt effected me deeply. So much so I gave this painting my greatest efforts along with some others to break the back of power so wrongly used.

Can you imagine Christ's pain, along with Mary's, knowing in that moment he was going and leaving his greatest love and coequal to continue with God's trust to mankind, knowing she was to carry forth a royal bloodline, but more importantly to continue truth, that all must be balanced, male- female. Love is the key to finding how this great lie created afterwards with fear as the oppressor, how fear could be used to suppress truths.

Christ's teachings were also Mary's, and her own words would have completed a very depleted picture, for already in those days humanity was beginning a very unbalanced road to travel.

Mary was to be the deliverer of God's light to the masses, but what eventuated was a travesty of justice and truth. Not only was and is the Divine Feminine suppressed, God's own perfect design was altered, pulled apart and dismembered to give an unbalanced fearful ideology to build religion upon. Anything built upon false foundations, and even more so when using violence and suppression of free will must fail.

My truth was this, love was and is the key, not judgment, not suppression, not an unbalanced world where the thinking of the masses of humanity has been founded on a false premise.

Truth will set you free. Within this painting I asked for an extra figure to represent the oppressive church authorities who constrained any freedom of thought . . a figure to watch over and report my every move to church authorities. The hand behind the knife belonged to the hidden threat behind Mary, that threat which followed her all the days of her life. I asked for this painting to be submitted in this form as it is given because I wished you to be shown. . truth, with all the love it was intended. Yes as my personal homage to Jesus Christ, but to my most beloved and honoured Mary Magdalene, a woman of immense power, strength, and courage so great it brought me to tears.

How could a divine woman with such a mission be so defiled, so reviled as to portray her as a prostitute to continue what was a lie?

Mary Magdalene it is to you I devoted this painting, and to the sweet knowledge gained through the lips of a woman, and to her offspring and soul offspring who continue now the story. Always has it been spoken off, prophesied that Christ would return, but truth is male energy alone is never balanced, and when Christ returned so would his Mary in another form? Always have they been devoted to serving God, and it is so now.

There are other issues spoken about with my painting, my works and secret handwriting, and how I hated Christ and his family, this couldn't be further from truth.

God so loved the world he gave his son and daughter to be defiled and their words of truth scattered to the winds. NO!

I, and many souls with knowledge have always worked to protect the Holy family, and to perpetuate truth. So accept please these words and listen to your own heart. It does not make sense that God created an unbalanced system - an unbalanced view of life. No, his design was perfect.

This is the essence of truth. You cannot found a religion on misinformation and deliberate stripping away of truth and have God's blessing, any more than you can create a world of peace with one aspect in power. The time for this time of injustice is over, and new energies flow, God blessed, to create a new mass consciousness where all life is honoured, all people, where all religions look at the distortions which have eventuated and perpetuated through fear over the masses. Fear will have to go.

I am Leonardo, and in this my greatest of all pains I am relieved, and thankful to this vessel who so bravely saw truth as needed. Expressions of thanks are needed by me to her, I say I offer you my vision for one more painting to come, the Mona Lisa.

Love is the key.
Leonardo da Vinci

A WAKEUP CALL.
CHILDREN - JEWELS OF THE EARTH SUFFER.

A gesture of goodwill is how I see my words being received; a gesture of love and understanding of the times you as humanity evolve through now.

I am Leonardo da Vinci, and I wish to speak now of a subject very dear to my heart, the love of children. How I have watched in great sadness, children, that most precious gift to life in many areas of the world suffer extreme poverty and sexual exploitation. It breaks my heart to see children, innocents, left unattended after parents are killed, or forced into armed combat - villages against villages, and religious divisions and cultural differences being the reason mass killing has, and does take place.

Oh the children who suffer tear at my heart for they are innocent, without any ability to defend their lives or innocence.

Of all the subjects which I could write about through this beloved one, it is the treatment of children which cries out to be heard. Life for many hundreds of millions of children the world over are now suffering, used as child slaves, or forced to carry guns and kill their relatives, other children, and to commit the most vile acts against others, and this scars the soul.

Oh these children live now in a world created out of man's obsession for power, power and domination, and wanting what others have. It is such a sad reflection of the real of dignity of humanity.

Females have long taken the brunt of this blind ignorance and rush towards oblivion. Now there is hope offered not by man, a man, or men in general, but by the love of the Feminine Essence now emanating from one Goddess empowered by her Father/Mother - God, to return the flock's home to a remembrance of the Source.

In my time I was not blessed with children or close ties, perhaps the one wish which was not fulfilled as Leonardo; was to know the joy of fatherhood. Work was for me then the greatest consumer of my total efforts; but children, and nature, animals I have always loved. My need now is to speak in defense of the feminine, and in particular also children, innocent victims of man's self driven desire for total power.

Many millions now suffer, are without parents and homes, living in filth without care and without hope of a better future.

My plea to all who are able to change things now is to open your heart to children, support them, and send funds to aid organizations to take them to safety. I cannot even begin to tell you how tragic is the plight of these little children. It is abysmally tragic that such violence and lack of dignity exists in their lives, but when considering the plight of femininity, and the lack of respect given over the ages it does not take a great deal of mental intelligence to see the writing on the wall is the decline of humanity. If there is a lowering of respect and support of the feminine then humanity begins to deteriorate, and descends into depravity, anarchy, and a hate filled world so far from what God created, and this was and is primarily a masculine driven problem. Lack of equality and balance is the major problem now affecting many countries.

The African continent and many other areas are depleted of all love and higher ideals, and the decadency of man is a problem only you as a collective can correct, and it won't be easy now. The decay has seeped too far into the very fibers of societies, of cultures, and in indifference and wholesale seeking for what others have; creates now third world countries seeing the opulence of rich countries, and a loathing comes, a lashing out, anger and hatred for life in general.

This is the inheritance of man, a world descending into poverty of mind and values on one side, and on the other - greed and need for more power. All energies out of balance, and gentle words of encouragement are all well and good, but I have the honour now of being able to speak out and to try to make a difference, so I Leonardo choose now to try to reason with you, to look to third world countries, those areas of the world now being ignored by richer nations, and say, you can change this, and do it by helping to create employment for those who starve!

Find ways of sharing the riches of the earth, and for God's sake save the little ones! Take them in, feed them, love them back to health, and stop this sexual exploitation of children, it is so far beneath who you as humanity are, descendants of God.

Do not sit idly by watching television screens; seeing wars and desecration and shutting off, because if you do then it will not be too long before this black despair spreads ably aided by lower of forces would love to exploit fear.

You stand at the threshold of a bright new age, OR a world you do not want to see come, it is there now being nurtured by indifference and self interest. It is there now festering along with apathy and a need to look out only for the needs of the self.

I am caught in a place of the ownership of some of those feelings of deeper sadness, for I Leonardo loved life, and love this magnificent planet and creations, and to see such a rush toward oblivion drives me to speak, not in quiet words of beauty, but truth. For truth I have always defended and always will, and the truth is; there is a great divide created and empowered by man, not women. A world with more feminine influence would never have ended in such a dire impoverished state. Women are the nurturers; they would not have allowed such vested interest to overtake common decency. They are protectors of innocence and dignity of all beings; in general women would not have allowed the world to descend into this state of despair and greed for power.

I appreciate the fact that man has had to evolve with a great deal of misinformation, but even this has been largely controlled by man. So now a precipice exists when mankind appears to not have evolved enough to cancel out the madness, and the only answer is the feminine must be given equality to bring balance back, but each and every one of you chose to be here now to make a difference, to wake up to your true heritage before it is too late, and to open the heart to all people, to start this evolution of thought and hasten the return of the feminine.

It is a saving grace that God the Creator has empowered His beloved daughter to oversee this time of reclamation of the flocks.

It is high time in my opinion that some dignity was returned to poorer nations of the planet, and the feminine restored to her rightful place at the right hand of God.

I am in awe of the majesty and beauty of this world, but a reality check is needed, soft words do not seem to awaken.

Perhaps then my blunt words will be received as I intended, that they may shock you into a realization time is short, and the opportunity to shift humanity out of harm's way is far too close.

The object of the coming times is survival of the planet, not what new goods can be purchased, and little regard given for others who also share this time on earth.
Leonardo da Vinci.

"OH WRETCHED MORTALS OPEN YOUR EYES."

The elementary pathway of learning is now open to all via the compassionate efforts of the feminine to hold all safe while humanity evolves through some troubling times. I am Leonardo; this pathway is offered that there is an opportunity to overcome habits learned over the ages. Chosen pathways become too embedded with anger, greed, and animosity for anyone different; and it would seem a limited life expression is there for all of creation whilst this violent and closed tendency continues.

I have seen a gentleness settle upon the faces of people who have started to assimilate this energy, and without understanding why a contented comes, a knowing that in spite of what appearances say by visual interpretation of the times all is where it needs to be for the evolution of the species, but this is not about humanity alone, and that is overlooked. Peaceful creations - those who just exist and do no harm are being hurt by the actions of humanity.

Evolution of the species would say; means survival of the fittest - to live and control the world, but it is this general conception that has this world on the brink of destruction; not at risk from other species, no! Nature takes care of that, balance is kept and thrives were it not for the interaction and manipulation and actions of humanity. In short humanity does not enhance this beautiful planet as they are, but quickly places it on the brink of disaster, and many millions of people, billions in fact do not yet see who they are. There is no standardisation of goodness and virtue at work - a basic structure of goodness and equality to base a civilization on. Humanity has in my opinion evolved in some areas, and devolved in many others.

What can be done? What can be done is to aid this ailing planet, bring awareness to everything you do, see the nature of goodness at work around you and amplify it daily. Initiate education systems which teach ethics and values, as opposed to religion classes which still perpetuate misinformation to control the masses. Evolve out of ignorance and aid others see the nature of goodness as a baseline for human interaction in all affairs.

Globally there are millions who adhere to goodness, and living right and this needs to spread, for humanity, in fact the planet to have any chance of surviving. I have seen what ignorance can and does do, it keeps millions of females, infants in perpetuity of living as a second class citizens without rights, and given little thought other than; what use man can put them to - what aids man's dominance.

"Oh ignorant humans" (mortals) I once said, "open the mind and evolve out of ignorance and violent tendencies". Life for many people is just this, and not wanting to repeat what others have said, I will instead speak of justice and beauty, and a world of such profound beauty in natural order - a world which now experiences man's greed in such proportion that you, and I use the term as a generalization of humanity, exact such great and deep designs on nature there is little chance now of you undoing the damage done to ecosystems, to the land and water systems. I pity the children who will inherit such a poor legacy! How will future generations see your collective efforts? With great anger and sadness I would say; that greed was the governing force for your collective evolution. A bleak world exists there now, a picture of a world of lack, of oceans depleted, soiled, and left with floating islands of rubbish and toxins seeping into it - a world where the land is so undercut to fill your collective lust for more fossil fuels and power there is little left. A bleak picture not one humanity can have any pride in.

I speak as one who has witnessed the passage of time, and seen some areas grow in light of understanding, and other areas decline at such a rate as to cause genuine concern. Many would see my words as cynical, as those of someone at a loss to see the goodness in humanity and the scientific gains. The true evolution of a species isn't to be judged by how many individual scientific improvements are made, and there have been many, but by the collective karma, the end result of your living on earth, and the collective evidence is tragic indeed - a species gone wild with greed, and a need to conform to group collective beliefs, some which clearly do not serve to make humanity more compassionate and caring. Some are downright violent and dark, and governed by lower forces.

The other Masters have spoken of various aspects of evolution, spiritual, climate, and educational factors of aiding enlightenment. I would like to speak of an area I do not see so much growth in, and yet little is done to correct this tendency.

I as an artist and lover of nature and the feminine wish to speak of the beauty lost, the life spark, creativity and spiritual delight of reaching up out of ignorance and finally becoming one with the Maker, not as in a lecture upon how God has been ignored, but out of compassion for the Feminine Aspect of God, a Creator of compassion and love. I see the pain which we all share that at such times as when humanity is meant to evolve, humanity now pulls away from direct connection to God and nature, in favour of collective activities variant to areas of the world - countries where religion is so heavily controlled by implied threat and violent tendencies there is little chance of breaking the cycle. Brainwashing so complete it is considered a violation of the law to question, to have a genuine thought, one counter to the governing bodies, usually men.

Femininity is at threat just as much now is in my day, only it has taken on different form. Love that gentle expansive energy has been completely overthrown it seems, and so is common sense. A world of exclusivity, of one belief, one set of for men and another for women is a very bleak picture, and I would be wrong to only speak of the positives. A reality check is needed to pull attention to this narrowing of focus. The feminine is just as at threat as this planet, Mother Earth, so I see this time as a direct threat to the feminine. I see a time coming when love is overthrown in favour of religious fervour which has no concern for the earth or the feminine, and it is a dark period in human evolution.

To those who think perhaps I should only think of the feminine as an element of human evolution, and not support one aspect women over men, I bring a counter argument; there is no better time to speak in defense of the feminine than now before all hope is lost.

Many of the messages have spoken of hope, and of love and optimism, but a reality check is needed to bring to your collective consciousness - the end result of this blind ignorance if it is allowed to develop; an outcome far more dark awaits, and it is easy for some to believe as men it isn't such a bad option to stay in power and to declare I'd don't care what happens later, except for one thing.

Remember please, a dark planet devoid of life and with little grace and love is a desolate future, and karma comes back to those who ignore wrongs. Life is a cycle of incarnations. One may come at one time as a man, but the next as a female, and so what goes around comes around as they say.

Life for all of creation needs the feminine, and it is my great love to defend truth and the feminine. I offer my advice, and words of praise for equality, also as a plea "wake up humanity before it is too late, and that slumber you stay in becomes a permanent period of life, without joy, and without beauty, majesty of nature and all that is good.

I stand for the Sacred Feminine - always have and always will. It is a deeper love which drives me to give these words.

Oh wretched mortals - awaken before it is too late, love as I do truth and defend it always.
Leonardo.

THE PURSUIT OF TRUTH.

Allowing for the growth of humanity has always been a problem for us, those souls who have chosen time and time again to uphold truth, and it will be my great delight now to speak of the Sacred Feminine and employ what skills I have to hasten her return to power and respect. Of all the pathways humanity could have evolved through; that path chosen and followed of masculine dominance is the most damaging of all, there will be a moment of recognition needed that there is not that fine balance within societies.

Harsh terms are used at times to describe the feminine, and an obdurate view given of love as a sideline to any physical relationship between men and women. Love as the central pathway of gentle healing and transformational properties allows any relationship to grow in beneficial light. It would seem to be a time now of seeing one side of life, but primarily from the masculine aspect.

Within this book we attempt to correct this imbalance by legitimizing the feminine and giving truths as we see them.

I am Leonardo da Vinci, some would see my name and say 'what rubbish that this scribe should dare to claim we who have always loved and revered the Sacred Feminine would write through her gentle hands', but the truth is, I, Isaac and Sandro have always loved, revered in fact the Sacred Feminine, and it is logical if given the opportunity to speak, to voice our opinions on such an important subject that we would do so. I am graced with a gift now to have my words received by one of openness and love, and I am most grateful, to her do I say thank you.

Within this book I wish to promote the pathway not chosen, one of a gentle journey of equality and love, and respect for the Feminine Aspect. I won't now speak as others do of the problematic path of modern civilization, but instead speak of that superb journey of discovery which was my life - given that I lived a life of contemporary views of the time only in a need to conform, at least on the surface. I lived for art and study. A burning need for truth drove me on – a ceaseless desire to know all there is of life - to render in pictorial form a graceful representation of life, and to know more of the inner workings of life, to the point I found joy in contemplation; in finding the truth hidden behind layer after layer of conformity - to old thoughts regardless of their truth or worth. I was relentless in the pursuit of truth, and found a joy unimaginable in simple beliefs not given the power of free speech.

Love that most precious of all energies was for me not in relationships, but in the correction of misinformation and historical distortions which slowed humanity down.

I have observed over time many trends; many advancements in knowledge and science, and with attitudes, but the rigidity stays the central focus for human interplay. Millions find they are disadvantaged because they are born into cultures or religions which devalue the feminine, and this we wish to change. How? By introspection of valued parallels in learning, and observation of corresponding periods of movement against the light of truth being revealed.

We wish to knowledge life's difficulties, but ask for your understanding of our passionate defense of truth. Some would say 'but whose truth'? Obviously we can only give it from the higher vantage point at which we observe life and mankind's evolution.

I as Leonardo was an avid learner; my mind sought out new ideas and concepts, and in a world of a dominant and heavily oppressed religious governed society; to walk the way of openness and light was dangerous in the extreme. I sought to bring truth forward to enlighten the ignorant, and to do this in whatever way possible, art - writing and scientific exploration and gathered knowledge, for knowledge allows the light in, allows growth to penetrate the very cornerstone of ignorance - fear as an implied punishment to holding views not upheld by the dominant religious hierarchy. I broke many conventional rules to support my truth, and along with others chose to find a path, one secretive out of a reality that to go against the mainstream religion at that time was considered heretical.

Mankind was ignorant of many truths buried and covered up to protect a very lucrative business, and to dominate through superstition and fear of punishment for believing differently, counter to public opinion.

The life of Leonardo, and many artists of the time and freethinkers was one of constant protectionism, lest we be imprisoned or punished, and to put death for disagreeing with dogmas and conditions not honouring freewill, or the feminine.

I chose the only option; to find others who also valued truth and free speech, and who like me had knowledge suppressed by authorities for centuries, knowledge which could have led to our deaths if revealed.

Life was not as open and charming as many feel.

Against all odds the truths we sought to protect have withstood the ravages of time, and been passed down to countless enlightened beings capable of sustaining life's influence, and who through it all are clear holders of truth.

Such efforts have been placed into the restructuring of many areas of life, and yet the spiritual aspect, the religious icon making and problematic transference of dogmas have in my opinion held humanity back, and pose now a great divide in human understanding which may take further centuries to remove misinformation and distortions.

I uphold truth that man is not the conqueror of the universe, but sadly has contributed to the defiling of the image and being of the Sacred Feminine, and none bar the Creator can really modify a belief system which is so entrenched, but given free will we who represent the Spiritual Hierarchy and support God's retrieval of worlds can do little but work where possible, and within the limitations of human understanding at any time.

Hence a dilemma, where one sector of humanity have and are evolving, and the other on the whole devolving, and becoming even more separated from God by holding a desire to orchestrate the downfall of the retrieval efforts. How by steering human religion and superstitions into allowing fear and masculine dominance to grow; enforcing even more rigid and non loving cultural and religious practices. This is not a singling out of any particular religion, but simply stating fact, that while some sectors of humanity dig more deeply to religious rules and dogmas which are restrictive, judgmental, and profess to follow a great and wise teacher - enforce newer manmade inclusions to control the population with fear.

This we fought against in our time, this ignorance, and sadly we see a reenactment now. Life for many millions of people is shrouded with ignorance and fear; a perpetuated cycle, and we can but work tirelessly to awaken the masses to God's – the Creators loving gift of free will being utilized, not for personal gain and world dominance of one country, religion and culture above another.

Little has changed in attitudes to women, and I speak in general, I do not make a blanket judgment of all of humanity, but single out those divisive and corrosive hate and fear filled areas of concern that you may see where change can be implemented.

There is need for you to do this yourselves, direct your course and that of humanity out of ignorance, and into the light of understanding all are equal, and all are loved.

My life as Leonardo was devoted to enlightenment and knowledge, and it is thus so still that I support all actions to awaken humanity out of ignorance, and it is my great joy to do so.

My inspiration was and is truth, and honouring the Sacred Feminine, so it was and ever will be.
Leonardo.

THE ULTIMATE ACT OF LOVE.

A gathering of light beings, those of high order have been orchestrating a retrieval of worlds under threat from those forces - energies which defy the Creator's Light and wish for the flock to come home. As one of those beings who have a part to play, I now speak of one area unknown to many now, the actions of the feminine; active efforts to correct what we in our time on earth could not accomplish.

A Creator God came to earth at another time, many times in fact, a messenger of Light, a son of God, and that is well known. The great avatars, Masters of Light, sons of God, but the misconception that it was a male only effort must be corrected. There were many attempts at the retrieval of humanity to aid them evolve, and in each case there was balance, always the feminine held equal power. Always equal, it was never to be the case that humanity accepted the Feminine Aspect or daughter of God, for that threw out the age old dominance of man - the stories of man's wondrous exploits, but never of the feminine as the one to hold all safe, and deliver truths equal to a man.

This is the one area I am passionate about; the defense of the feminine and God's right to have the feminine restored to her place of dignity and power. This has always been a sore point, and at this time in human history I rejoice that the feminine has taken it upon herself to deliver this influx of love and light.

Aphrodite, Goddess, Venus; she goes by many names, for aspects always aided one of the male teachers of greatness. Some you know; Aphrodite was also an aspect of Nefertiti, Bathsheba, Miriam and others, and always in every case written off as a whore, as a temper of man, but no more. In each and every case the feminine aspect held equal power to the male, but humanity was not ready for this, and so the male dominance continued. The stories remembered to reflect the wonder and power of the king, the profit, the sage, but never was accepted the importance of the feminine.

Even Lord Melchizedek who did not have a feminine counterpart on earth was supported by a flame, or counterpart in spirit beaming down energies to hold focus for him to achieve his task. In each and every case the masculine was exemplified as divine and be honoured, and the feminine of no or little consequence other than as a diversion.

Over time the Hierarchy in charge of the reclamation of worlds have thought, reconsidered actions, and seen the futility of repeating over and over again the action of sending a male retrieval team, a new avatar, and much of the historical writings speak of waiting for a male avatar, a Christ to awaken humanity.

A long deliberation took place, and it was considered that humanity had not evolved enough to repeat old patterns which just enforced the idea of God's preference for the male aspect. A dilemma came, one which caused concern - there was no answer which would not repeat old patterns, until a daughter of God, Venus or Aphrodite spoke up and said. "I would like to do this - to offer my services. The world needs one thing to bring about balance, to bring understanding, and awaken from the slumber of ignorance mankind. I will generate this love, and as love is the only thing which is more powerful than fear; love is needed. I will do this, take on this role of elevating the human consciousness to bring understanding back of the divinity of all life. I am love, and I give of myself", and so it is now energies are and have been emitted from the Sacred Feminine to bring balance back to humanity as it proceeds into these challenging darker days.

Why dark? For fear is well entrenched now in human consciousness, and a feeling of disconnection from the source of life. Love is the answer, and to all life now a soft glow of love comes, invisible, infiltrating all human conditions.

Dictators will fall not by the sword, but by the soft energies of love lifting the human spirit enough that all may start to think of freedom of thought and speech; where before military regimes held absolute power, now will come a dissolving from the inside structures out.

Aphrodite the Goddess of Love empowers positive change, and she is aided by her flame, she is everywhere, and her love dominates now all layers of societies and cultures. Freedom can now be sustained, but not without trial and opposition.

The task ahead of humanity now is to evolve, to awaken and recognise truth, to speak with respect of historical writings, but also with awareness they contain many distortions which do not aid with equality and healing an ailing planet.

A gift is given now humanity to heal and awaken, it is the ultimate gift of love from the Sacred Feminine, please honour it as such.
Leonardo da Vinci

7 MARTIN LUTHER KING JNR.

SOCIAL ETIQUETTE VERSUS TRUTH

Whenever two or more join together in God's name 'there I am'. This was a statement of truth given to aid the unenlightened at an age of religious superstition and guarded opinions, but it true today.

I came now to join these Masters to open a new energetic link in the evolution of the human species. I am Martin Luther King Jnr. and I have a gift to give to all those who will listen- love spoken in words of truth to aid with your transformation and elevation of consciousness into a new paradigm of thought.

Challenges come to all people without fail, all countries, all nations, religions and cultures, all are in the same boat- a rocking boat now, one about to tip into a sea of concern, and I say this without holding back, for words at this point of history count more so as every day goes by.

Love has always been my message, that and the love of God, but from my vantage point now I see no more time to waste with pleasantries. I see only an expanded vision of problems I witnessed in my time escalated. Oh yes social reforms have taken place.

Racism in America has had some champions since my time- those who remind humanity of the frailty of the human condition, but not enough has been accomplished to aid the Negro population.

Hurricane Katrina along the Mississippi coast and at New Orleans showed just how artificial is the concern for poorer people, those of different colouring or nationality, the poor, the black, those dispossessed suffered more. Help came too late for many people, and for some people it was impossible to escape what is mankind's socialised prejudice which is still deeply rooted in the hearts and minds of the population of many countries, not just America. I asked to begin this discussion group to really give truth to this most massive of problems- a world contrived, conceived and manipulated to keep the poor in their place and the richer more powerful individuals sheltered by laws, attitudes and closed thinking.

Australia made a move forward, and the reward was a lifted consciousness of humanity. The mass consciousness lifted, and a race of people breathed a little easier, with pride at last in themselves, and so they should.

Some people may think that as I am not in human form incarnate now, my words should ring with love and brotherhood, and they are. For the greatest gift I can ever give is to give truth through loving observation of what societal pressures and activities still keep humanity struggling with the have and have not's. Always the rich and powerful negotiate to keep power, not understanding that love of all people as one entity; one unit is the only way for survival.

Society, all societies are plagued with a 'NORM' which is created from perceptions and feelings of personal power and superiority over others, and none can deny that gross injustices have been perpetuated in its name, but now time is running out for humanity to shift out of those thought forms, and many may deny their own prejudices, but all have them to some extent.

What I wish to bring to the surface during these discussions is, life and liberty run hand in hand with personal success and feelings of belonging, of life being worthwhile. How many Nations of the world now struggle with world monetary funds and larger Nations manipulating stock markets and economies to keep the status quo?

We aim to start this discussion night with perhaps the most erosive of all human characteristics. The need to make others feel inferior and keep them in their place. I saw a child a week ago in a state of despair, and I saw a man and woman brush off this child as dirt and left her to grieve her family alone, and to starve at the side of the road, and I saw my topic.

How to have everyone look at themselves as compassionate human beings, and then look beyond the mask which is displayed to keep others aware of superiority. What is it that makes you so afraid of holding a child's hand and offering love, words, food and shelter?

What is it that generates this need to hold onto position and power at all costs? I have a challenge for each one of you, to look at this statement and answer it honestly from the soul, not the head.

How are you making life better, easier for others less fortunate?

What are you doing to change your own attitudes, knowing beyond that evidentiary evidence that the world will be an entirely unacceptable place to live in the future if there is not rapid change? Your climate tells you, speaks out loud and clear that you are selfish. You take more than you need. You do not put yourself out unless there is something in it for you. Now some people will be so offended to be spoken to in such a manner, but I do this intentionally.

Truth will set you free, but only if you face truth head on and start to shift yourself first. If anyone in this discussion room can shift tonight and open up and see the truth of my words reflected in their life so far, the world will start to shift, and the mass consciousness make massive moves in the right direction? I know I have given strong words, uncomfortable words, but hear them now. Speak from your soul. Let your heart speak, not the intellect, not the head and mind disconnected from the heart.

If I could change one thing about humanity, this would be my wish that all people are created equal and treated as equal. I would wish that no child suffers another day of loneliness and starvation while rich nations hoard, or hold, or withhold, and spend countless billions of dollars to perpetuate a war machine, keeping 'some' in power.

It is my wish; you as humanity see the error of your ways before it's too late. Some would say why take such a forceful tone, because truth needs to be spoken and shared by each of you with every person you meet. Not out of judgment, or persecution, or seeing yourself as superior. Just remind each and every person you meet how precious they are, every one.

Even the bum on the street, the child left homeless because of aids, those dispossessed because of drought and famine, and believe me there will be many more before too long, unless an over whelming movement begins, and for that to happen people need to wake up and be honest with themselves.

Love will keep you safe while you look at these questions, and I would ask you to look at the questions with total honesty.

Be brave enough to say, 'yes I have perpetuated a problem within humanity' and stop it. Stop this cycle of greed for power at others expense, and say 'Oh my God how I am so very grateful to be able to serve your sons and daughters all equally'.

If I could have one wish, one dream it would be this, that you at least see each other for who you are, magnificent beings of light who deserve nothing less than truth, a truth founded on love of God and each other as one.

I have a dream, one of humanity undivided by prejudice and power mongering. I have a dream that you will experience a movement tonight of divine revelation you are now called to a purpose greater than your daily lives and social lives.

I have a dream that by the year 2012 a new light will shine, far brighter than it does now, because a lighthouse is beaming its Truth out.

This lighthouse is your purpose, to ignite the flame of truth and power it up, so that no corner of the globe will be untouched by your light. Light comes with shedding, it comes when God permeates every cell of your being, and is broadcasted out, and as such the mass consciousness changes. Each discussion night another Master will choose a subject, a topic relevant to them, and during these discussion nights there will be many revelations, and we will through this woman, our chosen vessel give words to urge you into truth when blockages come up. It's now time to set a new light and cast out darkness.

Let us do it together, motivated by each other's bravery in facing truths. Let us all join hands and say we are not alone. We stand together.

Let us make it OUR dream that a better world is created.
Martin Luther King Jnr.

8 SANDRO BOTTICELLI

GUIDANCE FOR WORLD ECONOMIC RECOVERY-
BARAK OBAMA - ABRAHAM LINCOLN RETURNED.

Discrimination is by far the most divisive of energies, and with the coming years you will be asked by your soul to challenge yourself to look at and remove discrimination.

America made huge moves forward in voting in Barack Obama, but there is still a long way to go with removing this energy from humanities mind-set. You have now a President in America voted for by those whose consciousness have shifted enough to see that openness, oneness and inclusiveness is all that is valued, and it should be valued. You America have shifted, and in fact the world is shifting, but there is so much more to do; in Africa that war torn continent which causes more internal strife at the moment than others wish to acknowledge needs assistance, and it is in the throes of weeding out those extremists who use hate as a weapon to suppress and kill, rape and maim the innocent.

We who represent the Great White Brotherhood and Sisterhood of Light do care very much what happens and when, and we urge you all to now acknowledge this great and momentous shift in consciousness, but also see there is so much more to do to eliminate this from the mindset of Countries. All countries have to some degree discrimination strongly there, but the good news is this movement to love has gained momentum and grows so fast that it will not be stopped, but let me tell you what we feel is needed to continue this shift of consciousness and speed up the recovery of energies in Africa.

We feel there needs to be an economic package developed whereby more aid is given with infrastructure, as an attempt to aid self rule and empowerment of the African people who have been submitted to denial by wealthier countries. When countries are experiencing extreme poverty and lack of food, discrimination is also in force when no aid is sent. It is a case of empower the people, feed them, yes, and empower them with not only food but also self-pride with an infrastructure and the ability to lift their heads. All can benefit and the needless slaughter of innocents will end.

Tyrants have existed over time, but they always fall, whether it is in a short expanse of time or long depends upon how compassionate are others who see their problems and find ways to aid the people suffering, irrespective of the political slant of leaders, and even in the case of where a tyrant runs roughshod over his country. There are ways to empower the people without increasing violence. Love and benevolent views of their needs would help.

One who holds power by way of military might and creates fear will fall to his own actions, those who are within his own party will take the lead by peaceful means, and then we urge all nations to aid each other, to not exclude countries suffering now because of economic woes affecting the whole.

If you saw money as energy, and all exchanged energies out of love this does not have to be as serious as the circumstances indicate it will be.

I have asked to speak to you now through this vessel, because we see that not only the environment and economy is important now, but also how you respond to each other. If there is a global concentration upon setting up a more fair system for economies then this would flow on, would begin to ease political tensions in countries where strife is rampant and hatred has turned into a way of life. Treating others with respect is part of the survival package you as humanity have at your disposal, that and knowledge all needs to be seen now as part of the economic management package. Not just look at the individual, but how equality affects the whole.

What you have now is a golden opportunity, one with great implications, and disastrous would be that outlook of excluding those seen now as in poverty and having no say in the healing process.

Your world exists because you create it the way you want it, and instrumental in this present economic and environmental crisis is greed, greed for resources and greed for power.

A wonderful thing has occurred; a fresh breeze has entered into the political arena. A man has taken office who does respect all people, and we ask you to see this man as our choice, he has the potential to do great good, but he needs your help, each and every person on his planet to keep this planetary consciousness raising and aid it to continue, to see how you can help by letting go of any discriminations of race, colour, religion and economic snobbery.

Those who are experiencing poverty are not less than you; they are in fact brave souls who have come at a time and place to reflect to you wealthier nations a lesson. For they give you a gift at great sacrifice to themselves, they reflect to you the profound privilege of living in better circumstances, and the challenge is, do you see this reflection and honour it and say 'yes I see how inequality really makes us all disempowered'? It is a dilemma which many have fought with for centuries, how to respond to those less well off than you. Oh, many have responded with holding on tightly and not seeing the gift of love that can be offered, and some wise souls say 'this isn't right, let us address inequality now'! Our advice is humanity, take this golden opportunity to look at global economic problems not with closed view and hoard or pull away, but see an expansive view.

See that all can benefit from a redistribution of wealth. It is called loving compassion, and it empowers the whole.

Abraham Lincoln has returned and in new form, he comes to aid a world in distress, but he can only succeed with your help, all nations pulling together and forgetting barriers and old hurts.

It is the only way to peaceful coexistence, and it is preparing the way for Christ.

Blessings.
Sandro Botticelli.

RELIGION HAS IT HAD ITS DAY?

I speak now on behalf of those Masters of Light responsible for shifting the mass consciousness of humanity, and it is through the outer sheath, that energy body of each individual will the consciousness be raised. We are offering you humanity a chance to shift on mass to a new elevation of consciousness available to all, but declined by many for they stay within an envelope of ignorance of their own making.

Willingly do we come to guide you past this time of responsibility for your own evolution of consciousness, and willingly do we give you words and energy for this time of expansion of consciousness.

Blessings be to all who attend, and all who read these notes- a blessing for your safe arrival past these days of trial. I come with an urge to shift you at a particular time and strengthen you for your journey. We strive to have you understand your world consciousness is threatened now and even more so in the coming years. What you achieve now in planetary recovery and reinstatement of your own belief systems will aid you when these times come and energies are heavy with potentials not yet seen. Why so much emphasis on the mass consciousness? Because my dear ones evolution of your species into a higher framework of thinking is necessary.

There is a doorway of opportunity coming, open to all, but only those who have eliminated lesser energies may enter. A structured doorway is open to those wise enough to evolve and seek potential for the whole. Advance the cause of peace by finding peace within. You will not find peace within unless open to other streams of thought and expansion of consciousness beyond your present understanding now.

I come gift in hand to ask you to respond to energies and find your own understanding expanded. How can this come?

Discuss your evolution of consciousness, what does it mean? How is your consciousness expanded if not by opening your thoughts to others views and challenge the very foundation of where your beliefs come from, and the structured use of religion to keep the sheep controlled? To infer that religion per see is wrong and damaging for humanity for some would be heresy, but we wish to point out that without the rigid conformity of thought given by religions there would be potential for peace.

This statement by necessity would upset many people for the mass consciousness has been contrived to arrive at the point of discussion, and then stop for religion itself is a dead end. This is not to say magnificent beings, great deeds and much kindness has not come from religion over the ages, but also so much hatred, intolerance, judgment and blind faith in an unfriendly God, a wrathful God, and this is damaging not only to you humanity as a whole, but also strips away the individual's right to know God personally. Religion as it is must go. It is a scurrilous statement some may say to indicate religion is no longer needed, but we want you to remember this and put this into your mindset; the only way for world peace and for differences and divisions to fade is if religion disappears. What a statement, this would give some people panic to even suggest this that religion is damaging. Religion has held the reigns for so long, with boundaries of thought and implied restrictions that only damage can come if it continues.

Take the goodness and keep that, take the love and compassion and keep these, but remove now Oh humanity the need to see yourselves as governed, but rather take your power and direct connection to God and use this. See where the path leads if religions continue. Wars will come. One religion against another, reminders of the inquisition will come with fundamentalism breaking out, fear, constriction of thought and behaviour.

All these negatives permeate the human consciousness will proliferate and grow.

Look at Christ, at Mohamed, Buddha, at Gandhi, at any of those Great Ones who have urged you forward. Take the essence of their words, the love and brotherhood, the nobility of thought and remove the fear.

You have evolved humanity, and do not any longer need the restrictions of religions, they have twisted the human psyche to a point that no growth comes. Religion must go. Why must it go, because it is a limitation of thoughts to a point that individuals stay within the confines of thought and are often fearful of each other and of thinking for themselves?

How does it aid the human condition to keep it? What are the plus's and minus's?

What can you personally see coming for humanity?
And how can you help others evolve out of fear, and into a state of being where they are Christ or Mohammed?

How can you survive without religion?

How do you see humanity evolving, and into what? What is the future of humanity if religion and misinformation remain, that you are sinful beings and worthy of punishment by an angry God?

The subject is perhaps the most important one for some time, in that it will aid humanity to see beyond the limitations of thought now held, that you must have limitations for your own protection. This subject is indeed powerful, emotive and threatening for some people. Religion has had its day; this is a subject very important to the future of your planet. Divisions were never meant to be there. God sent his messengers to aid humanity evolve past limitations of a particular time, but these same limitations have been imposed by those who control religions.

Oh yes wise men have given words at times, but so much pain is instilled, so much fear and mistrust and a feeling of superiority of one religion over another, and the Ascended.

Masters weep at the pain perpetuated by closed minds meant to hold the population in a state of fear, for control over the masses comes from keeping a fearful structure in place.

Some will be aghast that we offer a suggestion that religion has had its day and the only way to peace is to have no divisions between humanity, and for love, compassion and the essence of any of the great teachers to be retained. LOVE ONE ANOTHER AS I LOVE YOU. This should be the universal cry, not Christians against Moslems, one religion against another, and while in the background those who seek power and have no connection to spiritual values, or what some see as religious passion seek to overpower the population.

Religion has had its day, and what will come will come, but you are powerful individuals, all capable of free thinking. See the potentials, while some religions vie for power, those with a need to oppress will take over. How can this be a just cause to leave humanity without a religious Hierarchy? Do you need a Hierarchy? Instead take your power back and respond as individuals with love, compassion and justice. Seek to promote the best as human beings and pull together, and know that peace will come with Christ when He comes into his time of power at a critical passageway for humanity, and He will offer you no religious directions. He won't set out rules, but empower each individual to shine. Over the ages his wise words have been appropriated and twisted and used to create a power base where individuals rule by imposed fears of damnation.

Can't you see Oh humanity that you are not sinful at heart, your soul is pure and you have the potential to do great good or to let the lesser side, the ego take over. It is our hope you will see before it's too late that love is the only teaching you need, and a healthy connection to God, whatever you consider Him/Her to be. Let the barriers fall, instead of Catholics, Hindus, Moslems, Sunni's etc consider yourself to be a son or daughter of God, and see each other as loved and honoured and know peace will come not from keeping barriers there out of fear and seeing others as a threat, but dissolve the differences. Love them as you love yourself and your planet.

The course is set, the road ahead comes, but peace will come not by holding on so tightly out of fear, but allowing peace to come through love.

Please think about this subject and let your own limitations be seen by you and remove them. We are there for you as you shift this most divisive of all subjects, Religion.

Blessings
Sandro Botticelli.

ON FUNDAMENTALISM.

When any real shift of thoughts comes to humanity, counter moves also take place, and so it is today, just as it was in my time as Sandro Botticelli. Willingly did I confront day to day thinking of the masses, but rigid was the thought form, controlled, without freedom of expression unless you were an artist, and this gave but a little more freedom of expression.

Decisions come and go and life goes on, but through it all one thing is constant, as it should be, the need to shift humanity into freedom of thought, respect for others opinions and forms of belief, so very different.

What to one is deep regard for God, seems to be tantamount to fanaticism in others, and this is the aspect I would like to address within this discussion group . . . fanaticism in its many forms. Where true belief takes on an ugly turn and collides with others free will. This issue is very dear to our hearts, we who honour freedom of thought and free will.

Blessings come in many forms, and there were once upon this planet wise men and women who knew the inexhaustible energy which could be harnessed for good, and so religion began. Innocent at first, a meeting place to share sacred views and beliefs, and what flowed on, then became religion in its many forms. None of these wise men and women, the avatars who gave concepts of God's will into human thinking, did they see how what was innocent wisdom could be utilised to feed agendas, or how their own words of wisdom from the One God would be altered, decapitated and truncated, to reveal with time religious off shoots.. . belief systems bordering on obsession to conform.

Such constrictive energies have inter played, to dance upon the waters of truth, to contort and bring through oppressive, structured thoughts with little in common with original truth . . simplicity, love. purity and joy. Little of this is within current religion, fear based, rigid thinking dominate, male patriarchal heavily over toned views abound.

Femininity, at one time revered for what she was, the Feminine aspect of God, has now come again into density of form to combat the growing male dominance and fear, and what does she clothe herself with, but truth. In Birth Of Venus", the Goddess, the muse dance about with joy. One of the muse offers Venus a garment of joy, pure light and joy. She is then clothed in abundance, balance and clarity, seeing through the eyes of one having been washed clean, but she is offered a cloth of abundant joy.

This is the blessing of this time , that joy so lost, so pushed down and hidden is now given again. Rejoice in life. Do not look through oppressive eyes, and try to deny others free will to voice an opinion, see this as needed. Joy is on the move again.

It enters humanities mass consciousness daily, and never before has it been so needed.

Fundamentalism is one of the most potentially alarming problems you as humanity are to face. It is your own creation. Fear drives joy out, innocent laughter and beauty begin to fade under the boots of fundamentalism.

Listening to your world media, read between the lines, watch media now rarely speaking of truths universally. What free country now has freedom of press? Financial implications are real for control of world media. He who controls the media, controls the world. See those areas where religious fundamentalism already begins to creep in, into politics to aid with domination of one political and religious bias. See where the infringements into civil liberties takes place and speak out.

Freedom of thought, free will is God's greatest gift to all people. Do not let it die, slowly and then more rapidly being replaced with secular beliefs only dictating what one is to believe. In my life as Botticelli, I lived a life not perfect, but I did honour free will, and pledged to walk a long journey to express others rights to freedom of thought and speech.

Recently I heard the words, "If you are not with me you are against me" as an implied threat, and in this I saw the next big threat, religious fundamentalism and religious domination impacting upon world politics. Choose your battleground they say in cloaked words. Hardly empowering free will with any delicacy to democratic rights of individuals to freedom of thought.

You live at a time of greater change and now this change speeds up, creating a vortex into which will pour all of your energies - continue with such aggressive language and bully tactics and you create a faster decline for the loss of vibrational frequency.

Listen carefully please to my words, you have been given an opportunity as never before, the Goddess, the Divine Feminine is being released into your vibrational frequencies to aid you pull through this episodical period of confrontation. How does it help to ignore the dignified speech of eloquent men and woman, to portray the backyard bullying language? It doesn't, what this does is to deplete all efforts made to aid you and your planet now. Joy, laughter, compassion, diplomacy, and sweet love will heal your world and lift you to new heights.

When given this opportunity to speak about lifting the collective consciousness, I could do no other than to approach the most difficult aspect you face, political and social pressures to conform to religious fundamentalism. It is the greatest threat to humanity now, for its heaver overtones do not promote love of all, compassion and grace. No! it suffocates the life essence out of your potential as God created beings.

Given the opportunity to speak, my greatest joy would be to aid the return of the Goddess, one I have always worked to protect, and this I do with so much love.

Compassion for others views means you do not have world leaders creating a vacuum into which can only come fear, and issue oppression of free will. Love is the key to this and many, of your problems. Creativity of thought is everyone's right, and expression of those thoughts given power gently do raise the whole. Perhaps the greatest joy, Christ, Mohammed, Buddha and other Avatars gave was an example to follow, gently, never bullying any other to promote your own ideas, thoughts, and dreams, and deprive the world of a Golden Age.

I thank you for so receiving me, and I urge you to think about oppression of others with words or implied force, it is destructive indeed.

Sandro Botticelli.

DISCUSSION AND TRUTH.

You need now to achieve a level of understanding of how discussion breeds growth, for in opening of the mind so too does the heart open, and the flower of love begins to bloom and create within the Psyche a new energy matrix where before closed minds and hearts meant that no growth could enter now comes an explosion, an expansion of consciousness, the light of understanding flows in and what then occurs is an expansion of one's energies and aura. Then closed energies which held out new colours, new vibrations then expand and you expand in energy. You become aware, and more open are you to others.

This matrix then builds to incorporate other vibrations, and so as if seen as an image you appear to be brighter, lighter and more colourful, but the energies linking you are so much more profound.

"I and my brother are one" is one of those parables given to humanity at the conception. You are all brothers and sisters of all beings regardless of religion, colour or creed, and this discussion group has developed to initiate a new energy for you, but also to unite you to all of humanity and your soul.

Without introspection, reflection, there is little growth, but now we enter a period of rapid absorption of energies, given out and received, and there is little doubt that you will never be the same again.

This discussion is different as you will be initiated into your own understanding of who you are. What do I mean by that? I speak of generous souls who see themselves as willing to change, to open themselves to growth, and to see where light has been diminished by holding onto less than positive aspects of personality. Reflectivity becomes permanent, and you reflect to each other aspects of the whole you were missing, you are gifts to each other of truth.

Truth shall set you free they say, but so many do not want to hear truth, they find it unpalatable, uncomfortable, and somewhat distasteful, for the ego is confronted by this challenge, but what we see as essential to growth of humanity is an openness to create a venue, a place where truth is the only thing given or expected. Truth given with a loving heart is not only a gift, but a blessing, for often truth is burnt upon the pyres of conformity, to stay hidden, to be invisible, but do you know you cannot hide from the master within. The God within is shunned whenever you hide your truth so that you seem acceptable and lovable by others. This is not new to you, we have discussed truth before, but I wish to point this out, for truth is something you give each other only rarely, and with such caution it is often painful to even look at truth as needed.

So let us say this is all about TRUTH.

We spoke about what it means to be a Melchizedek, to what it means to walk the way of truth, but now we want you to think candidly about how painful truth is to you when delivered and you are rebuffed, actually punished by society for daring to be so bold as to stand by your truth. The reason we ask for this is that as you reflect upon the pain of speaking of truths we will work on this with you and give you energies to aid you in removing this pain.

For this process to work we ask that you look at how you feel and release this fear of speaking out, for you all have it.

You all carry a burden around that you will not be loved and then be ridiculed and then ostracized by society for being you. We will aid you remove the pain which you have held inside, and we will grant you energies to aid with this . . . one step cleansing for this discussion group is all about cleansing of the fear of growth, of being different.

The world you live in is precious, so precious, but also so loved are you. Never before have you had such energies given to aid with stripping away that which no longer serves you.

This about love being the crucible for pain, to release it and heal it and any division which has taken place. During the next few months' energies will shift again to allow truth to flow. Already ethics has been perpetuated and enforced with energies, and the ethics train rolls on, but what is impeding humanity now is lack of truth and an understanding heart, where love is seen as all important. How painful is life in the physical, but how beautiful too, and how much more you can grow with the opening of the heart to allow truth a place. Truth will set you free, but it isn't an easy journey. You will have found just how much opposition there is out there to truth. So let us utilize this time now to heal this with you.

How do you react to others when truth is not spoken? How do you feel now? What difference has it made to others when you had the courage to speak out, and what if anything was gained from this?

We ask you to listen to think, and identify how humanity has been encouraged to dismiss anyone who is courageous enough to speak out. In what way have truths impacted upon you? Truth can be painful to give it and receive it, but by far the most powerful gift that can be given is truth, for it opens the individual to growth, both the giver and the receiver. Truth will set you free, but some would say "what if another's truth is not my truth, or it is given from and unhealthy space, you can still grow from it"?

What is important is truth isn't feared. For centuries religions have hidden behind fears, in many ways when the original truths and so essential blessings and wisdom given from the heart of God into the inspired minds of wise ones has been distorted and hidden away, because many felt that they were the only ones who could determine if humanity were ready for truths. So consequently truth has been consigned to the background, and anyone who was brave enough to speak out to protect these truths were persecuted, and isn't that what society still perpetuates today, with a subversion of truth, where few live their lives honestly in every way. So much effort is put into keeping those with an open mind shut away, afraid of what will happen if you speak your truths.

This is the time where truth will come out one way or another, for there will be no closets to hide in, and the truth of it is fear is a trap. The only thing to fear is fear itself. Humanity has reached a time of cleansing. This has been happening for some time, first the ethics train began to roll, now it's the time of truth, and no nation, person, or leader, will subvert truth any longer.

An energy shift has taken place where truth is set free, and from this humanity will be lifted into a powerful new energy where nothing is hidden and everyone is respected, but the growth pains will be felt far and wide. The beauty in people, the beauty and truths in religion will at last be seen once stripped away from the masks, the misinformation placed to hide power away from individuals.

This time is all about reestablishment of truth. Painful but beautiful, and out of these three years will come a new Jerusalem so to speak, a humanity where all the divisions begin to dissolve, and a new belief will come that all are equal, and a unification of humanity will grow, no religious differences.

Isn't that worth the pain of revealing truth for the masses? Christ is here on earth, and as one of the Masters who guides humanity I ask you to see the joy which will flow when all are set free from the confines of religious oppression, to see each other and be open to each other as equals, with truth as the sword you carry, that and a loving heart.

This is the blessing of this time, that a new energy comes, truth, and the Melchizedek Order has released this, now it is yours to carry, but with a compassionate heart.

Sandro Botticelli

THE EVOLUTION OF MAN.

The challenge to domesticity and intellectual pursuit of knowledge is often hampered by a given attitude of superiority, and that superiority exists in a generalized view of man.

I am Sandro Botticelli, officially the attitude to woman in western society is one of decreed openness and support of a reflective view of compatibility of skills and attributes which broaden the skills pool of society, and a polite respect is shown, laws are in place against discrimination, but this united movement of expansiveness and attitudes to women is flawed.

Not all share the equal opportunities of employment, pay and advancement.

Some would expect changes to come slowly to man's attitudes, but I would prefer to see the state of feminism and equal rights this way, and I am Sandro Botticelli, or this is the personality profile you would identify with. In my time as Sandro I painted symbolism into my work wishing to relieve the pain experienced by women. I saw and still do the feminine reduced to an obsessive need by men for a possession - one cast aside when they did not and don't please; and succumb to the rule of men.

'The Birth of Venus' was my attempt to make a statement about the position the feminine has had over time, but a new concept; being born out of the ocean came a vision of loveliness, but one of power. Upon her shell she stands unashamed in her nakedness, with a vision of the future possibilities there, a wish you could call it of how I and others wanted the world to change - to see the feminine as divine, pure, and powerful, not hampered by the lower aspects of man's perceptions.

Aphrodite is that inspirational motivation for this work of art, the power of women adorned with purity, softness and power. This was not just a fleeting moment of artistic wishing, but a point of view held by many intellectuals, that the un-evolved, uneducated amongst humanity are easily led, and are fed lower energies and lustful thoughts to keep humanity at the whim of low influences. A crowd is easier to control if they can be aroused with thoughts which hold down a sector of society - of a scapegoat given to oppress and persecute, and that opinion many held, that the lower energies governed the evolved, uneducated, and so it is today.

I would like to handle the aspect of evolution in the periods of establishing a free and equal society. It is easier to reason with someone if the mind is open, if there are not preconceived ideas drummed into the mindsets, and education of humanity is fundamentally important in understanding where limiting thoughts come from. How a whole culture can begin a downward trend and perpetuate it because it empowers somebody at the top, often one who benefits from the ignorance of the masses.

Many areas of the world now as in my day are uneducated, live in poverty, and unable to provide for the family, put food on the table, let alone think of establishing new ways of thinking, and this malleable mass of humanity are managed more easily with violence, and this tendency is there well established in human endeavors.

Much of the world still exists in ignorance and significant poverty. In many areas women are second class citizens, and open to communal abuse and violence. I now have the opportunity to see from a higher viewpoint what keeps humanity locked in the abusive masculine dominated societies, and cultural aberrations and lack of decency.

Some would claim that 'they know no better', have had no good example set for them, so continue on with violent oppression of the feminine, but in truth it is easier to continue on with lower aspirations and tendencies than to stand up and be counted.

Long has it been told that 'man was to conquer the earth', not a mention of humanity. It has always been projected that Biblical account of man being created, and women, the feminine, as being an afterthought; created from the rib of man, and so misinformation has been fed to mankind since the inception of belief instruction, and religious beliefs taking form.

It is an institutional belief system of instruction so inbred throughout humanity, that in fact in my opinion it is a miracle humanity has evolved as far as it has.

People are not taught to think for themselves, to question, and formulate beliefs based upon logic, let alone decency and nobility of thought. The ignorance of man is the problem, and to this day many still preach these words, and promote man's superiority over femininity.

My vision of femininity rising from the ocean, washed clean of man's perceptions and limitations still holds firm, the feminine is divine, pure, and chaste, and the perceptions man brings to her evolution do bear some scrutiny.

Education of the mass of humanity is made next to impossible when such poverty exists, where the western world lives it seems for exploitation of the environment, and greed for market based economic wealth. Yes an evolution has taken place; the feminine is regarded as at least given the illusion of being equal, so long as she doesn't want equal pay, fair working conditions, without sexual predation by males.

The world exists now as a living example of the processes of restrictive thought, told over and over again, with views tainted in some way by the need to promote a particular point of view. I may sound to some as critical of the evolution of man, and in truth I am. Man has perpetuated a selective myth to this day which now creates the world at the brink of war like activities, all because it was easier to oppress and restrict free thought, that it was and is to elevate the feminine to her place of power, equal in every way to man.

One area I find of great interest is how the illusion of man's image has been projected onto God - that God is a fearsome male image, judgmental, vengeful and definitely male. How this is justified bears closer scrutiny, so I will speak of this when given an opportunity to do so.

We who in our time loved, revered and protected the Sacred Feminine do so now, we speak at last free from religious oppression finally able to voice an opinion, and how grateful I am for this opportunity.
Sandro Botticelli.

A NOTED VIEW OF GOD

Countless generations throughout time look forward to a new understanding of God, but how can mere mortals comprehend such a magnanimous energy of love? Humanity is governed at any stage by the current state of the world perceptions and evolution of consciousness.

At one stage there was a period of understanding which needed to be expressed in common terms, (the name of God) the Infinite, Master of the universe would not work because God's creation is as infinite as the Creator. So perhaps the greatest understanding human beings will ever have of vibrational resonance so above the conscious vibration of humanity; is to leave the general assumption there - that old perception the Creator is male, has characteristics of a male, and so the perception came God is a he, not as she, not a neutral gender, but in reality is both incorporated into energetic form.

Love is a vibrational energy hard to describe, let alone understand, so perhaps I will for all intensive purposes call God; not he, not she, but Creator and leave it at that, and this way the wrongful description of he won't be added to as the timeline of humanity aligns for a realignment with this benevolent Source of all life.

An active imagination may even be able to find a common word all feel at ease using, but for now God is a generic name use commonly around the world, with the exception of a few religions which convey a different terminology. Allah is to Muslims that divine word assigned, but this isn't my concern the name of God so much as the misunderstanding that God is male, and all attributes of the feminine has been removed. The Creator was robbed of the Feminine Aspect!

Those who have an understanding of energy would see the common sense in ascribing the positive and negative polarities to any energetic functioning. There cannot truly be power unless there is the function of moving energies between two points, positive and negative. Even the terminology assigns the feminine with a common word – negative - but one seen as less, as evil, or lacking goodness. Positive indicates good, and negative the opposite, but God the Creator of all life is a mix of, if you will both positive and negative polarities, hence movement causes vibratory resonance and movement.

Creation stems from the thought, the intent of the Creator to experience life in all its forms, and to see this creation develop out of love into something great. Perhaps then the greatest miscarriage of justice done was to deny the Creator the fullness of being, and place human limitations thereupon.

Many people will deny there is a Creator at all, they cannot perceive of a God of love causing or allowing so much pain, but this is where ignorance still persists to this day. God - the Source, created, and life flowed and evolved, and still does to this day, ever changing, evolving and growing, but when created all life was set free to evolve and develop in whatever way was necessary, and consequently freewill was also given, and that freewill is the greatest gift, and the greatest limitation.

Why limitation? For once given, God and all who serve the Light, the Source of all energetic life cannot stop free will, and all who serve the Light are limited, we cannot stop humanities wrong actions - nor death wish it seems by perpetuating violent tendencies.

Perhaps then the accumulated negative perceptions have a life of their own, and what you call evil is acted out daily by those who deny the Light, and that means denial of love, for love is all the Creator is – infinite, blissful, beautiful love in the form of Light, a vibration so high, so pure, none could contain or hold all this energy without destroying the physical body.

The Creator's son and daughter have held this partial light, but they cannot contain the power of creation within their atomic structure, cells, and RNA, DNA.

There are two pathways humanity is following, those who uphold goodness, light and virtue of kindness, and those obsessed with denying the light, and this is where humanity is now, with a world divided. Those who love and work towards a better world; and the exploiters, those who see personal power within their grasp, and who do misuse wealth, energies, and their time to create a false persona, one of power as a challenge to the Light.

It isn't my place to speak of that one who rebels at God's Light; I just wish to make a comment that God has been denied the feminine, the Shekinah. The feminine has been removed from the most honoured of positions at God's side. We who do serve the Light of love – the Creator, deem it necessary to see where this is going with humanity, and aiding where possible awareness of the feminine, and in this book and website Goddess Awareness, it is my great joy to add my words to reclaim power back for the feminine, and to address ignorance where it exists.

Many noble beings now fight to restore human rights around the world, and it is well acknowledged the feminine has been at the losing side of human rights and efforts. Today I stand counted and with pride state - I Sandro Botticelli stand for the Sacred Feminine, and deem it necessary to explain; your world is in desperate need, so much so an unhealthy state exists where ignorance and the masculine have lost the plot to use colloquial terms.

There is little contemplation of the implications of decisions, and far less effort placed into restoring the feminine to her place of honour than needed.

I wish only to say; gentleness is lost without the feminine, change is needed to a system of world dominance, and it must come soon, and the feminine is restored before it is too late!

There in is my wish and hope.
Sandro Botticelli.

9   LORD MELCHIZEDEK

THE LOST WORD(S) – SACRED-FEMININE

A moment of reflection gives this realization; life for women has been made unbearable at times - being those given attitudes of male superiority. Within this book are a compilation of messages for the Goddess Awareness website, but more than that it is for the enlightenment of humanity that we now relay all messages into book form.

Over the ages femininity has been given the road less traveled so to speak, restrictions have held femininity back, none more than the gross violations of human rights which have occurred largely because of those driven beliefs that men are superior, stronger and chosen by God, and we the Spiritual Hierarchy have not helped with this attitude.

We who have attempted many times to lift humanity out of barbarism and savagery, and we knew that ignorance and male domination was set in, we knew to send a woman avatar would get us nowhere, and humanity would reject such a gesture of God's grace. So we conceded to a degree and thought the only way we can lift mankind out of ignorance is to do this gradually, to show a new way very gently by introducing truths through men, but we also knew that in the process women would still be held back. We had no choice but to enlighten mankind slowly, and as the mass consciousness evolved we could issue more, show more, but such a tight hold has there been over the tendencies of man.

Power was seen as all important, love that very feminine aspect was denied time and time again, until humanity evolved enough to incrementally introduce energies to aid you to evolve.

At this point of time we stand poised at a particularly volatile period where the joyful exploration of new horizons comes with an edge to it, a question mark attached. Man has held dominance and power over human evolution for so long bringing change is harder to achieve, unless we the Spiritual Hierarchy instill love for the feminine with energies pouring down upon you from the Creator to restore balance and truth, and the truth is religion has an enforced view, well enhanced to keep women in their place. To send a feminine avatar before now would have resulted only in her death, and little ground recovered of consciousness raising, so we have utilized the period now being enacted, where a culmination of energies are there to aid humanity with ascension energies and planetary alignments. This was and is the most magnanimous of times to instill truth and restore the feminine to her place of grace and love. We have aligned just such energies now, and we now need you to understand the importance of this endeavour.

God has been denied His feminine aspect or counterpart.

To some God is male, a fierce being of domination and power. At one time God, Creator of all there is was recognized as balanced, as the perfected energy of love, but along this timeline of humanity, ignorance, religious dogma, and personal issues, and greed for power have meant the feminine was removed. God could not have a feminine aspect, and so a downhill trend came where power was man's right, and the feminine was and is denied. There came a revolution where for any woman to stand up and have thoughts voiced, to show power or knowledge meant a vendetta was carried out, and history shows the plight of the sacred feminine.

God was robbed of love, the most powerful ingredient or energy, and so it is now a division comes, a point in human evolution when we stand counted and say unequivocally, "the sacred feminine must be restored to her place of honour in humanity's history".

We have watched as millions of innocent women, girls and babies were killed, defiled and given inhuman treatment to keep this lie alive; that man is superior. Every day, even in western society women are denied equal rights. In some countries women are beaten or raped to deny them a voice, and the world you live in is in a state of poverty, not economic poverty, but this is certainly there as part of a cleansing.

This is a time of the return of the feminine, and a cry goes out across the world for freedom, countries who have not seen freedom now go through the throes of unrest, and change will come, and some so entrenched in male domination will fight hard to keep this there, and clamp down even harder on the feminine. The Taliban is one such energy or movement which endeavors to suppress the feminine, but throughout the world this suppression is still there, and everyday now this energy for positive change is now beamed out to you. It flows across the cosmos to restore order and love.

To rebellious worlds, those where darkness has entered the hearts and minds of people there comes a new light, a new transformative energy, and clearing out not only economies undergoing a cleansing - the mindsets of men also undergo this change.

Whether you fight this or flow with it, your world will never be the same again. No longer will you be able to hide in ignorance, religious dogmas and ideologies which suppress the feminine. Change comes, and just as minds open, some will stay closed. Some areas of the world where women and girls are seen as second class citizens, a new energy will impact, and to some male dominance is worth fighting for.

Centuries ago the inquisition killed countless millions of women and girls, and even cats; because they were associated with women. And as a result a plague came, people were not evolved enough to know cats kept rats and mice in check; and so a plague came to wipe out many more millions from disease, but my children the dis-ease is still there, bred into your global thinking that women are corrupted vessels that have power to tempt males, and therefore must be suppressed. It is time for a change of attitude, and now we issue energies to cleanse this dis-ease, one which keeps you as humanity locked into male dominated violent tendencies.

You as humanity enter now the most precarious period of your human evolution, because these war like tendencies stand at a conjunction of time and the elementary passageway of life will be offered up to war; and feeding of this masculine tendency to shut the heart and block out life, but femininity holds the key to the survival of your species and this planet. We now place all energies into restoration of the feminine to her rightful place in history.

We break trends, no longer will we come to a man only to enlighten, but show the way primarily through the feminine, love will be restored to her rightful place because God wishes it so!

There has been a dominant thought held that women are not strong enough, too emotional etc, but this is now seen by us as something to embellish, and love, that softer and emotional aspect has power in it, and make no mistake there will be a shakeup, and man will depend upon the female not to wipe his boots and cook meals and provide for his sexual fantasies and needs, but mankind will depend upon femininity for survival.

We have come to a point of time we stand poised to aid you humanity, when choices come to go the way of darkness or light, mark my words and hold them to be true; it is in restoring the feminine to her place of honour will humanity evolve and survive, and with you this magnificent planet.

A time comes when confrontation, war like tendencies comes to the fore, and the feminine will hold you safe. What you do with this choice is up to you, but the end result will be we will not tolerate violence descending upon a planet and rendering it lifeless.

You are the most evolved and magnificent of beings even as you are the lowest, but you miss the prime factor, the equating energy for power to be restored, the sacred feminine.

In this website and book are the messages to awaken, to restore power back to humanity, and an understanding you are more. We in these messages steer you out of ignorance, and into the light of understanding you are more.

During the next few years vast changes will take place and the Internet will cease to be a vehicle for widespread dissemination of information. Why? Several reasons, global events, solar output and possible war impacted events; should you choose this foolish course; it will be in the printed word only in the times to come you will have access to these words, and others by my partner for writing these words, and it is out of love and generosity of spirit we write this to aid you.

Please be aware the feminine is under threat in many countries, the very physical and spiritual safety of the world hinges upon you changing your views towards the treatment of women. No woman should be forced to endure mutilation so a man can have pleasure and a woman not. If a man cannot control himself; perhaps the place to look is at the bestial attitudes that are not healthy - loving instincts of a man for a woman.

A woman and females in general are not commodities to be bought and sold, to be subjected to sexual slavery, or to be kept hidden beneath the suppressed rags of man's loathing for his own lower instincts.

Love is the governing force with relationships, not mastery or power held over women, and if I sound to you concerned for the lack of nobility in how women are valued or treated, it is because I am. It is so far from what God wanted; a balanced, perfectly balanced union of minds, hearts and bodies, both equal in every way, just with different component pieces, but both complete, a perfect union if honour is given. Love is the key.

May I speak of the unspeakable topic; religions have told you are beneath you - that are sordid or sinful. A relationship of equals is what motivates life, a love so great both are empowered by it, and love doesn't always mean sexual fulfillment of desires of one, but what is best for both. A constructive relationship offers a kind heart, vulnerability and trust, and a gentleness, and yes passion, but passion does not need to be physical. Passion can hold a relationship together if a common goal is held, of family, of dreams fulfilled, and difficultly overcome.

All have a perfect counterpart, all even God, a divine aspect and we are no different. We who serve humanity have all ascended, found balance and integrated both masculine and feminine aspects, to complete the most powerful energy of all - love.

We like you have counterparts. One soul was divided, to come together at the most divine of all times - ascension and completion of journeys, and we do this together. We are not all powerful male energies, but balanced, and we have learned we are better together than apart. We, and our counterparts also serve God's Light, and we do so out of love, but you also humanity, all those on earth, each one has a counterpart, a twin soul to complete one, and to some very lucky souls some may think, a blessing comes, when that special soul touches your heart and there is nothing like it, but make no mistake love is there for all whatever life choices, whatever life deals up, or your soul chooses. Some will find twin flames only to find they are in impossible situations, brothers and sisters, mother's – sons, relationships between which can go nowhere.

Why, what could be the advantages such relationships?

Obviously they are not meant to be romantic. May I explain why such impossible relationships come - to teach lessons, to present to the souls new insights into loving relationships and service, for when it comes down to it, love is the glue that holds creation together, and it helps to understand that love is not just romance, but having the greater love for the loved one means lessons are given to help them achieve a new level of love and understanding.

Twin flames are after all created by God of one soul, which is divided into two halves of the whole, male – female, and without the other completeness does not come. It explains why some find such pain in human lessons which are not understood while in body, not all will find their twin flame, some are in spirit, and one maybe in body, but all can find love, and love it is which is the ultimate lesson for incarnating on earth, to learn who you are and come back to God complete; having learned the lessons the soul set for you.

I have a twin-flame who sustains her own path to serve the Creator, but in a common need to aid humanity, all do, and what is missed in this movement on earth of treating women as chattel, or possessions, or sexual slaves, is a loss of that ability to find completion. The further you as mankind go along the path of masculine dominance and seeing separation of the genders, the further you go from finding that ultimate path to God – completeness, in service and love.

There are people who have never found a person on earth to complete them, and they either shut off and cease to look at love; or they chase with a fury the sexual road, and don't find fulfillment of love beyond the initial output of energy, and are left more alone and cynical than before.

All may not be their flames, but soul mates are there, people who have chosen before you came here to help teach lessons, and aid with physical and emotional closeness and it is still love! Love is the key ingredient, love, and it is through love and balance one finds the fastest and surest path to God, to completeness. Some have sought love through sexual means, and use of chakra system to have this orgasmic energy flow, but if love is not there, it is still just a mechanical way of achieving a sexual act. I am writing of this, for sexual attitudes and relationships have been a major reason humanity wandered down so many roads which bring disharmony and pain.

Love is perfected energy of nourishment, enhancement of others energies and merging of perfect energies of balance, and many would feel it beneath the Eternal Light of Light to speak of sexual matters, after all religious teachings have avoided the subject, or told you, you are sinners, and so unworthy, and sex is a lowly act. No not at all, love is God's design for creation of new species, but also a way of uniting and embracing male and female energies, and thereby bringing healing and love to both.

Love is perfected blending through a nourishing of the energies of the beloved. The wrong would be if there is selfishness, and a callous attitude to have what one wants, and disregard the comfort of another. Love is the key, but the pursuit of love, and sexual seeking or power wrongly held over the feminine is a major problem in the world today, and humanity cannot evolve until this is cleaned up. Sex was never meant to be a weapon to take power, to suppress to make another feel a victim, or to use as a weapon of war, and this I will state now, God created man and woman to be partners, to share equally the upbringing of children, to hold a safe space for all to learn self imposed lessons.

To rape and to commit incest is to decry the very noble nature of your creation, and though God does not judge, you as humanity upon leaving this existence, your souls judge and determine what was not done well, and choose to come again and again and again until through the wheel of life you learn why you are here - to love and to remember who you are, and to treat all of creation as divine perfection, therein is God honoured.

I have through my beloved partner written over many years and given words and urged humanity to change, but you come to a period of time where your capacity to hold to love will be tested; to hold to noble motives, and see justice is served, and to let others defile God's creation does bring some very heavy lessons. All of it created by you, but I am here now to say, the 'sacred feminine' is that lost word, the secret knowledge many have sought without much success, and it is there now is clearly shown as I can put this, until the feminine is honoured humanity cannot ascend on mass; while there are pockets of hateful energy, cultural norms which exploit women or girls, or female babies - the ability to achieve perfect balance is lost.

The lost word is 'sacred-feminine' please restore it to your vocabulary and lives and watch attitudes to femininity around you, and in the world at large, and do not be afraid to stand up and defend her, she is so worth it, and God wishes it so.

Blessings
Lord Melchizedek

METATRONIC KEYS - LIGHT ENCODED ENHANCEMENTS TO LIFT LIFE – A BRIGHT NEW DAY COMES.

A challenge comes to all beings now to enhance the vibratory rate of the planet, but also grow in light. A very recent alignment of energies took place which now impacts upon all life, as RNA, DNA and the atomic structures change their coding. A great gift has been given to speed the forward movement and light enhancement of life on this magnificent water world called earth, or to some Gaia. We ask you to be aware that this structured reinforcement of light was beamed forth bestowing upon all life a new vibration, but you as humanity are only part of the life component of this planet, and as all life is integrated, interconnected, all life will shift at the same time.

How will energies affect you functionally, and remember that human life is important, but no more important than animals and all living creations and the earth, Mother Earth herself all are transforming, and the development of this light quotient depends upon the assimilation rate of individuals, and how open or closed are your energies. Pronouncements of light variants are made because all beings are different, unique, but made essentially of the same matter formulation for each species, all being an integrated part of the genetic and life patterns of this planet and beyond.

How will this Metatronic light enhancement affect you? Any one of the following symptoms from very severe and long lasting; to slight and lasting only days. The fact is all life must be lifted, and there are no exceptions. Light is given in love; a direct stepping down of God's love to make life enriched with a greater significance and meaning, but also a realization of the interconnection of all life throughout the cosmos. This is not only interplanetary but inter-dimensional, and so the most powerful light encoding of the Adamic seed given. So very powerful, and for some especially painful to assimilate and process.

If you suffer or notice any of the following, accept with gratitude God's Light encoding your physical being, accept that it will take time and possibly some rest and understanding to allow the transformation of your bodily form, but also remember animals will also be processing these energies at the same time as humanity, in fact all life will. The symptoms may be fleeting and so slight it is hardly noticeable, and for the sensitive souls and bodies the impact far reaching and pronounced. We cannot give you an exact formula for each person, all are unique.

- Bodily tensions.
- Discomfort of the skeletal features and muscles.
- Discomfort of the body.
- A feeling of pressure of being crushed like a vice has been squashing the body.
- Dizziness, inability to focus and think.
- Extreme tiredness for no particular reason.
- Confusion and a feeling of not quite being of the earth, or spatially aware totally of surroundings.
- Inability to get words out.
- Pain for no reason, such as the sore body.
- There may be nausea for a short or prolonged time.
- Headache and neck and or body ache, and other symptoms unique to individuals may be present, do not panic it is a natural process.

As this energy change has been the largest and strongest yet, it now impacts upon all life. There is not one life form or nonlife form which is not affected in some way. The important thing to remember is if you feel any of the symptoms relax, assimilate, and headaches which may affect driving or working heavy machinery, do take care, and where possible drink water 1-2 litres per day to clear away toxins and make this assimilation of light easier.

We do not suggest that every ache, pain or symptom is only as a result of changes, obviously common sense is needed. Take precautions look after yourself, family, and animals. Be gentle with each other, and if people are not well, are irritable and non responsive to your words accept that they may also be going through a massive shift, and need compassion.

This is a great blessing to be so lifted and prepared for a greater light. If you normally suffer symptoms of illness, or are in doubt as to whether there is a physical ailment, of course seek medical help or advice. There is no one on this planet or beyond who is not on some level integrating this light. Some will reject it because they hold to lower energies and reject God, this is their choice, but they may react, be aware of that, and that some people who are unstable, or taking alterative substances may react in an adverse way.

This process can go on from a few days to weeks, depending upon the light quotient properties of individuals.

This is a gift of supreme love from God, given through Lord Metatron and stepped down to a level as to not cause injury to life; just to transform life into a higher frequency, and as you can imagine, as the body is structurally transforming it can be uncomfortable for a time, but the end result will be a new life structure for all interplanetary life, one more conducive to love.

Actions to ease this process can be:

- Rest if needed to allow the process to continue –
- Some gentle exercise to our allow energies to flow through the body, and help stop energy blockages and,
- Plenty of good light food, healthy food and water.

Have compassion for anyone who does not process this easily, for some it will be painful indeed, for some because of extreme sensitivity, for others because they try to reject the light. One thing to remember out of this is you will be lighter, more brilliant and luminescent and stronger, and more easily connect to higher energies and God when it is needed.

Be aware Mother Earth also must process this energy encoding and transform, and this may be impactful with climate events. We are with you every step of the way to ease your way.

Our blessings are with you for this most joyous and most important of all energy changes.

Peace be with you.
Lord Melchizedek.

OPTIMISM SOFTENS HARD TIMES.

Upon the opening of energies to direct the course of future directions for humanity, two things occur; we who serve God and are of the Spiritual Hierarchy consider all the implications human freewill can take, we observe the very nature of people, and we see a chosen path which may be improved if we send energies out to aid with planetary awakening. The second course which may be taken is when there it is a need to determine a direction not in the best interest of humanity where we see greed and integrity compromised.

Many times a venture develops whereby the peaceful course for humanity is altered but our hands are tied, we serve God and we aid humanity with love and guidance, but there is a point at which we cannot pull you back from the course you as a whole choose.

In happier times I have heard people say. "We could do this, have this, be more open and flowing, now jobs are tight, economies are about to crash, and despair is everywhere." "Where do we go, and what do we do when the world heads toward such a precipice?" "We as individuals have little sway over the great mass of humanity." "People in high places make all the decisions, we are just puppets guided by the government and big business into corrals of thinking. We have seen better days!"

I would say yes at times things may appear bleak, but this is all illusion. You are what is important; you are the really important ones. You have the opportunity to change your existence to one of joy and hope, just by changing your perception of the world.

The world is experiencing a changing of attitudes, and it really is a good thing to see changes from an optimistic viewpoint. Yes economies are in trouble now, but this isn't who you are. You are divine. You are noble beings of great integrity and light, and you can change the world overnight if enough start to love and not hate. If you all see yourself as divine, and divinely blessed your perceptions change. What looks like a bleak picture can turn into a vision of possibilities, of love for other creations starting to be the important thing, not riches, not greed for power and exalting the ignoble.

A cleansing is occurring, and you are given two directions, both with freewill honoured. One of self pity, panic and fear, or one of seeing change as an opportunity to see a new way to restructure systems which no longer work, and which destroy this planet.

You are magnificent beings of such potential, pull together as one, and bring hope to the world. The world needs your positive energy and insights. It does not aid the world if you as humanity give into corrupted systems; and desires to outstrip other countries or people of dignity and sense of purpose. The world needs you to hold a positive focus for the whole, and if even one person reads this and decides to hold a positive focus for the whole all starts to change, and that is needed.

You as humanity have created a planet in crisis, I cannot deny this, but so much goodness and positive growth is out there just waiting for you to utilize these opportunities to create a better world. One where there is no greed and power struggle.

This is a message of hope that you will see beyond your own personal circumstances, and you can and will help others with a bright outlook. Love holds all safe while you awaken humanity, I Lord Melchizedek hold you in a safe energy to allow this awakening to take place, but it needs you to reach out and take opportunities for growth and move forward with joy in your heart, that you are so very loved, and you are!

Profound blessings are with you.
Lord Melchizedek.

10 THE SACRED FEMININE.

A PLEA - RETURN THE SACRED FEMININE TO HER PLACE OF POWER.

Around the world changes occur and bring with them some upheaval, but in most cases it is a good thing, especially if it frees up human equality and graceful return to love in all things. I am drawn to write now through my beloved scribe of an issue long seen as the major reason your planet now is under threat of aggressive behavior and responses less than compassionate.

An imbalance occurred some long time ago, the place of love at the side of God - the Sacred Feminine was written out, and in this position a male only energy was supplanted, and with this a descending spiral for humanity. Oh, we have spoken about this before, but this is now a pivotal time in the consciousness raising of the planet, and with an expansion of energies a gift was given into the hearts and souls of all beings; the capacity to change, to move forward, and be open to new ideas.

Feminine rights are hot on my agenda now, for I now see this as the major factor holding humanity back. Male domination has been a limiting force for centuries, but with a gift of love a child was born, and I speak now of another time in history, one very dear to my heart as Jesus Christ - I speak of equality. I sought to break the back of old practices, of male domination in place to this day. May I say here unequivocally God loves the Feminine aspect, so much so He gave me as Jesus Christ the opportunity to remind His children of balance, of the greatness of women - born to suffering and ignorant beliefs that a female child had no value other than that of a price which could be sought, and then sold off - in some cultures seen as worthless, and in others the feminine was taken as a child and used as a slave, a virtual slave to the whims of man.

Oh the pain this has caused us to see this practice survives so. To redress this situation I was born, but I was given a helpmate so to speak, one of feminine nature and brilliant mind to share my teachings with, and overtime I devoted my time to share truths with those who were able to generate forward thinking. To my disciples did I give my words of love, but also included women in my enclave, my higher initiates, were many of them women of high intellect and knowledge, but to one did I give my role or was to at a time of great pain and trial. My mantle was I to leave to my beloved - a woman of noble birth, but also dearly loved by me.

Was this seen by those of fixed mind as right action? No, some, Peter, was against any woman having such a place at my side, at the side of a man, and to one so feminine in her capacity to love and share knowledge did he find trouble accepting her with any form of respect.

I include this here now only because in fact throughout history the belief has been placed that religion, spirituality and higher knowledge was only ever meant for men.

Oh my children this is so far from the truth, and the energies given now open you as humanity to a new insight, of women - femininity as needed to restore balance, and hold an equal energy. In this time Miriam was my right hand, and she held lessons, taught, held classes for others open to learning.

The time came where my significance on earth was to be tested, and for this action of leading the flocks home away from male dominance and corrupt religious beliefs I was persecuted, and was part of my significance, but my beloveds, the point was lost. A royal legacy was lost, and a new pathway for humanity broken.

Was I as Jesus Christ here to start a religion, NO! Just to point out a new way of looking at life was needed, that love of God was needed yes, but 'the Kingdom of God was within', that the road was not of harsh judgment and pious sacrifice, but love, gentle, sweet purposeful loving practice of living and being thy brother's keeper, and who holds such a perfected sacred space for nurturing love?- Femininity!

Oh, of all of my existences as Melchizedek, or my other aspects, I have only ever pointed out, 'the Kingdom of God is within', that 'to love one another as I love you' is the only way to live. I will not now speak of the crucifixion and beyond, for this is beyond time now. Of all of the pain I suffered in this time, nothing gave me more pain than the way Miriam my companion was treated.

In a moment of grave resolve I saw that she would suffer as I did, and worse because she was a female, and some will find this hard to believe, because humanity has firmly placed Christianity as a male dominated system. It was my beloveds my greatest pain, that out of my concern for her welfare the course was set for Peter to take this role and run with it, and the course of history is now seen, but what was lost was balance.

Was it my weakness that I could not allow one who was to inherit my mantle from doing so out of concern she would suffer a fate worse than mine? Oh, of all the concerns this was dear to me, that this woman of such grace was not given the chance to show her strength to the world, and so it is today, a long legacy has been generated where women are seen as the weaker gender, but beloveds, no man could have ever held knowledge and love and deliver them as she did. When all is said and done, she was to deliver into the hearts and minds of people our words of love. If that course was taken she may have been persecuted and killed for the right to deliver God's truth to the world, but what would have occurred perhaps; a shift - a shock may have gone out that the path of mankind had turned to such barbarism and women hate.

We will never know, because the mantle went with a man, and the course of human history, and but would the world have changed? Would the balance of truth given through the words of a woman have changed human history?

At this I have pondered along with other Masters, and we have thought, has a precedent been set up that flows on and will not correct itself easily? Was that moment of questioning the strength of courage of a woman one major mistake? I can but speak of this as an observation now, and say, how much of human life now is set around a role for the feminine beneath a man's gaze; other than as a possession or sexual object?

Humanity has evolved, but the pain is still there beloveds, and I can tell you it is never far from my mind as Jesus Christ or Melchizedek, that feminine rights are what were sacrificed.

Oh, it may be seen as a noble thing to some to not put a woman at risk of physical pain and persecution, but perhaps it was not fully honouring the power and majesty of femininity, to deny her and all women kind the right to equality. It is ever on my mind as I watch now across the world, women subjected to violence, and seen as a possession to abuse or confine.

There is such fear of women - of femininity, and therein is my pain. Had I the strength to hand that mantle which was always to be hers given by God, would the course of life now be different? I can but say, old habits die hard, and perhaps all of history is encapsulated in this time now, where freedom flows across the globe and the thirst for more, but what of femininity? Until the Sacred Feminine has been restored to her place at the side of God, pain and imbalance will continue, and there is great wisdom in loving life with gentleness.

Some countries now exhibit rapid change, but others keep women trapped, dominated, subjected to strict codes of dress and behaviour now which do not conform perhaps to the next phase of planetary cleansing and this is the most important of all aspects, and it is my sincere wish it is - a cleansing of attitudes to femininity.

Whether humanity is ready for it or not now, the feminine does reclaim her rightful place at the side of God, and with respect for the power she holds.

Those cultures which are so afraid of her power will now begin to loosen the hold, and she will at last begin to shine as she was always meant to, as dearly beloved of God.

A plea comes from my heart, return the feminine to her place of power.

Lord Melchizedek – Jesus Christ.

FROM A FEMININE PERSPECTIVE.

Many people would not understand that it is possible for Lord Melchizedek, or Jesus Christ to share their feelings and thoughts with me, but it is entirely so. I have felt His pain on many occasions on witnessing the lower aspects of mankind, and also in a discussion with a group of people where through me Jesus Christ spoke of his pain knowing a decision he made out of love and compassion for his beloved, altered the course of human history.

It was not his personal mistreatment and abuse at the hands of his captors which held such deep pain, but that he loved so deeply his beloved he did not want her to be persecuted, imprisoned, tortured and killed fulfilling their mutual task and fulfilling her mantle. Her path was denied, not because he didn't believe her worthy or to be strong enough, he couldn't bear for her to suffer. It was a compassionate act of protection and love, but the results were that a woman was denied the right to show the world another way; her love of God and that women are equal to men, and if necessary to reflect back to humanity their repressive and violent ways by giving up her life and that of her unborn child.

It was the ultimate act of love to want to protect a beloved one, but I wonder how deeply this denial of her spiritual rights and integrity as a deliverer of Gods message would have impacted. Let us just imagine the feelings of this woman, chosen and empowered by God to fulfill a task, how she would feel, disempowered perhaps, confused and hurt, even betrayed? She must have wondered why, once again the feminine was denied her ability to choose, and once again a man was given this role. I feel her pain, and now women, girls the world over have the impact of mans superiority, enforced ideas of what the feminine is capable of, and I weep for the loss of choice.

From a feminine perspective I can but write of life as I see it now, of joy and living in a country which at first glance respects feminine rights, and in most ways this is true, we are granted some respect when we strive to conform to life as prescribed, but even in a progressive country there are limitations. A woman can expect for instance that equal pay is not automatic, and still many workers suffer with expectations they are not quite up to men. In business the glass ceiling that women can reach for is still there less than men's.

The rights we in Australia take for granted are seldom seen in other countries, there are millions of women around the world subdued by violence, rape and torture, and suppression of rights is standard behaviour, and the right to free speech denied.

I am so very happy that energies now are opening the ugly can of worms so to speak of inequality to allow in that breath of fresh air, but is it enough while anywhere on this planet a female child or woman is denied human rights, and then all suffer. Religious freedoms are nonexistent in some countries, and cultural etiquette will not allow a woman or female of any age to attend male dominated ceremony. Segregation is rife, and little if any freedom is given to a woman or girls needs to be seen for who they truly are. Those judgments made centuries ago are still in place excluding women, and religion enforces this with a denial of equal rights.

A woman can't be a priest, can't attend certain male dominated ceremonies. Organisations still exist that are exclusive to men, and there is some free will of course to exercise choices, but is it going both ways? When is it now correct to ask a question of religion, 'why don't you allow female priests or women to hold higher office? The answer is a religious paradigm is in place, that woman are not up to holding higher truths, but to look deeper beyond the rigid conforming to these old behaviors; the answer is the same. 'It's a man's club', women are not good enough, intelligent or strong enough to hold an equal space, but do you know, we are!

We have the right to freedom of dress and behavior, and so long as this does not minimize standards of society, and does no harm, how can it hurt to embrace fair play?

Long ago a decision was made to write out of religious writings any power being attributed to women. Women were seen as evil, the tempers of men, even Miriam was branded a prostitute to discredit her. Women were and are seen as not capable of sustaining a discussion; female talents were restricted to being submissive, and allowing our wishes to come out only if it pleased men.

This is not a discourse on displeasure with men at all, but a statement of intent that we will not be held in that vision empowered by men, as a woman is 'to be seen and not heard' and other such limiting judgments. Women, femininity is here to stay, and no longer will we accept a castoff role, one of a lesser role than men. We are equal to, and we are changing even as men are changing, shedding, and across the world because of energies now being projected into creation - the feminine is being restored to her rightful place of respect.

Yes pockets of rigid male beliefs exist, countries or regions and cultures will still fight to keep the 'men only mentality going', but just as freedom now is fought for, equality for females will now permeate all levels of life, and a softening come, but do not expect this to be a time when women will fight as men do and suppress, and become ensconced in dominant groups.

A softening comes now to all people, no matter what country, and an opening of systems sometimes with greater pain and difficulty for a time, but it will come. I have heard the statement used so many times in relation to men's wars and aggressive behavior, now this statement has a different ring to it, there will be a softening of attitudes to femininity, to the Sacred Feminine "because God wills it", and therein is truth.

Aphrodite - Venus aligns with a moment of transition to expand the consciousness of man, and to open it to a new understanding, "we stand with you at your side equally"! Love it is called, and it is not a threat, not some sinister move by any lower influence to sway the might of men, it is just a blessing from God; one which says, "I need the feminine restored to her place of respect and higher energies".

No more images of Eve that 'wrongdoer' who brought mankind into sin, but now a new image, one correct and not corrupted over time; where all life is balanced. Males – females, equals in the face of God and a flow of love from a much higher aspect, that of the Divine Feminine finally being restored to her power.

This will be an image worth holding onto. A world of peace is offered, upheaval may come whilst she is being restored, but she will be, "**because God wishes it so.**"

Blessings
Virginia

FROM THE GENTLE LOVE OF A CHILD.

Great deeds are created out of love for the noble intent of mankind, at times the gentle, the loving are the stronger memories, so I would ask my beloved partner to write after me of the year which evolves now into the most remarkable by far.

2012 already has many taking notice, climatic events, climate change and political upheaval, but you know the most memorable moment so far this year has been the observance of love entering into so many areas of growth.

Of all those seen one which touched my heart and brought a smile, that of a gentle little girl who took a leap of faith and flowed forward with her desires for joy for family and friends, and put aside her own needs; to give more of herself to ease pain caused by financial stress. Such a little thing and yet so very powerful, for it is indicative of the nature of this child that she hears her father's voice, and not as a booming voice from the heavens, just as a gentle warmth deep within that warms her soul and it helps it stir into an awakening. Already this little girl hears the voice of the soul to become a healer of nations, and she does this her own way.

Some may wonder in writing of the year 2012 why I speak of the noble nature of gentleness of a child, but my beloveds, this child is awakening already, and when given her mantel from God her father, she will begin to take up her role holding this magnificent planet safe, not safe from all the changes which will now come as a significant signature of humanities folly and wrong action - this is there now as part of a cleansing of attitudes and damage done to the earth. No, she will gently emit a light to hold a safe space for humanity to evolve into something greater. No longer will that blind rush to towards oblivion be there, but a softening comes; like a soft mist covers all life and a healing energy comes, so graceful and so beautiful balancing all it touches.

Will this miracle mist of light stop man's aggression and love of war and hatred? No, but it will soften, make a transition possible where before there was no chance, now they will be, so I am ecstatically happy this child - unknown to all but one or two, will begin in earnest to balance this world and aid Mother Earth in her own ascension.

Many are of the opinion the world ends on the 21st of December 2012, no not so, but this year is extremely important to the planetary cycles, some of which are unprecedented and monumental in importance and influence, but this year will be fraught with anguish for many people, for there is little understanding of the time of awakening. All great periods of evolution come with upheaval, but it is not all bad as they say!

Many aspects of humanity need to change, you are a dangerous species as you are now. Humanity has at times little humanity in it, and the rush towards destruction at your own hands is there as a definite possibility. You have free will, and we must honour that, but it does not mean we who represent God are willing to see lower influences destroy a brilliant gem in the heavens, a magnificent water world, unique and perfect.

We cannot interfere with free will, that is the difference; with lower energies there are no such noble intent, power and self preservation is all important and anyone who gets in the road suffers, that is the difference with light and love, we work with your soul permission to help awaken you to the monumental times you are now living in, and alert you to your power to change your future. How by guiding you into more loving ways, we soften the hardness which captures man's desire to succeed at all costs. Love it is called and it now secures your future. Not by taking power or stopping human actions, but gently emitting a light from a Christed child, yes a female, even as a male also evolves to take a place in human history in a very different country, in a very structured surrounding.

Balance is there to aid you in future times, it is God's gift to you to help steer you gently through some very troublesome times. I speak of the times to come, but already this energy is held, and the feminine brings balance back now through the influence of Aphrodite, Goddess of Love, her energies now hold focus for safety to ease and soothe the passageway for all of light - all of God's little ones, even those who are unaware and who do not believe in God or Aphrodite.

So great is our love we all send you energies now to awaken and soothe your days, some feel this as a warmth - a feeling of being surrounded by love, and some just a feeling something is happening but they can't put their finger on it.

Love is here to stay, and right now we hold all safe for the evolution into a bright new day, a day humanity evolves and can shift to ascend in energy, and create a world of love and oneness.

Will this magic day occur this year one could ask, and I will say, oh my children the rate of awakening has been slowed over the past fifty years with many influences not wholesome, so know it will not be a mass exodus, on mass from this timeline into the new earth. It will take longer to achieve, and this may upset some people who expect a mass lifting of humanity this year, or a final battle of darkness and light, but no it is a gentle transition my beloveds into a new way of being, just as Jesus Christ indicated a long time ago, of light being revealed to every living soul, every creation with an explosion of understanding of the divinity of life, all life!

So pain may come, but know you are loved, and we are there to aid you, even those who do not love the Light and God are helped when needed, for there is still light in all beings, and God wishes his creations to come home.

This year will initiate greater changes structurally to your planet as she cleanses and protects herself, and to you are given energies to aid you evolve, but political, societal, and protection of this planet are all meshed in a cleansing of epic proportions, but it is all good, remember that! Even the hard times will be eased if you can keep your heart open and be your brother and sisters keeper. Goodness is what is revealed through these events, yes the worst is seen in human beings, but Oh beloved's the beauty and majesty which is you, the real you stripped of pretense and false illusion of material grandeur, you the real you, a being of perfected wonder is there, and such a grace will you reveal when others suffer.

This is a golden time of opportunity to become something greater, divine beings on earth. Oh it is a time of great changes, but see yourself as stronger than the events which may come to test you, and become a brilliant light for others to follow, not from words given, just a noble example of all that is good in humanity.

Love seals you for these times of discovery of your own soul intentions and why you came here now at this particular time in history. Make your life count, be that noble light others wonder at, and remember that example I gave of a little girl, evolving into the brilliant jewel she is, the feminine essence of love, pure and gentle, and holding all safe for this evolution into something greater.

Profound blessings to you for your journey.
Lord Melchizedek.

DRAGONFLIES - BREAKER OF ILLUSIONS – CREATORS OF NEW REALITIES.

The noble nature of our lives is often not revealed until presented with events or occurrences which test the very metal of our being. At first glance one could say of life how hard it is to be here on earth at such an eventful time, but to those wise enough to listen to their hearts, the souls real intent for life becomes more obvious; why such choices were made by the many billions of beings who have incarnated now to be such an important part of these crucial days.

2012 has started off with challenges, and weather unknown to us, so used to weather that was predictable, but no more.

We strive to understand why at times we could actively choose to come at a time of such upheaval and testing, but now I have seen the evidence before me of life in the fast lane being so hollow and non sustaining, and seeing people crumble when life presented them with loss of prestige, belongings and home.

It has a way of humbling people to see the very frailty of a system based upon materialism, and let's face it much of the western world operates upon what is fast, easy to access and eat, and move quickly onto the next distraction. Life for those same people is handled so differently if one identifies the accumulation of wealth as being the sum total of their being and identity; how easily the world crumbles and all the known signposts to security are gone.

This I have seen with one person crumbling totally, so identified with position, possessions and appearances of wealth the self was lost, an empty existence exists, whilst for the husband who didn't identify with positions, boats and supposed wealth, dealt with this so differently because he knew he was an individual with skills and intelligence and a soul purpose, and so flowed into this transition almost with a comfort to be relieved of the burden of such accumulated possessions.

We are not our possessions and wealth. We are divinely blessed souls who chose to be part of this great expansion of consciousness known as the golden age. There are so many people who plunge into despair when presented with difficulties, but with an open heart and seeing how other's needs are important, the emphasis upon self shifts also, and love for the welfare of another can help ease personal pain. We are all evolving, some slowly, some without any effort, and it is all good, even the tough spots because out of it illusions are broken.

My greatest joy has been to be part of nature, and remove attachments to material possessions. Non attachment to outcome can be a very liberating feeling; for one is freed from the consciousness of having possessions, the mind can soar to perceive much more subtle signs of oneness and the beauty of life.

A dragonfly blessed me with alighting upon my hand and stayed while I talked and worked. I said "thank you for the blessing" and it departed, and it was a blessing to be part of nature, to experience life with an open heart and inclusiveness of all creatures as divine. Dragonflies have always been a great love of mine, along with frogs and eagles. Dragonflies are the breakers of illusions and the creator of new realities; so perhaps this is indicative of why we have all incarnated on earth now, to help break the illusion of separation from each other and other creations, and our Creator.

Perhaps what we are beginning as one to do is create that new reality, a richer vision of the world where love for each other, and creation is more important than that illusion we live in - that we are separate to God and each other. It is my belief this attitude is why mankind has been lulled into a false reality that we are nothing without prestige, jewels money and possessions. At such a time as this I find it so beneficial to remove as much of the superfluous goods and possessions which overwhelm our lives, and to give to others.

We are alive at the most blessed of times, testing yes in more ways than one, but it is good, all for good purpose to help remind us who we are in relation to each other, the earth, and the Creator of a life.

I am not a religious person, I have sufficient soul memory intrusions upon this life, reminders of other lifetimes where I incarnated to remember who I was and make some sort of difference, and in those times pain was experienced; especially female incarnations at the hands of religion, so I am acutely aware of the soul lessons for coming this time.

Each lifetime we come with a soul purpose, though we have no memory of this in body. Rarely do many retrieve other lifetime memories, though they can intrude upon and confuse present lifetimes, but in all I have been shown; six previous lifetimes and the lessons I came to learn I saw where mistakes were made, or where strength was needed to be developed this time, and it all makes sense to me like pieces of a puzzle.

We as a soul, as divine creations come in ignorance in an effort to remember who we are - divine beings and aid others also remember a connection to each other and God. In this existence materialism and greed and a false illusion has clouded humanity, and was leading us down a wrong path, one of false values.

We are unique and beautiful, no matter who we are, or where we live or how much money we have, we are uniquely, divinely so.

A little dragonfly also came and sat up on my shoulder, and I saw a massive eagle soar above me but look down and acknowledgment was there one to the other, one of the most impressive experiences of my life, but that is another story of the connectedness of life.

We are more than presently seen, and out of hard times when tested and pressed between hard places our true heritage and strength is shown, and in these times with an open heart we can create heaven on earth; we create it every day with loving action, and graceful remembrance that other brave souls also chose this significant time on earth to be part of this great awakening.

We have so much to give each other, so much joy and laughter, and in hard times hope is needed and is free. We can all be an instrument of hope on earth by remembering the divinity of all life, and aiding anyone in need to our best ability, and if you have little give a smile and a pat on the hand and a kind word. It costs so little to aid others who have lost hope.

I have learned what I am here for and having seen other lifetimes what did not eventuate and why; I work to honour my soul and my Father Mother God by upholding love wherever I can, and it isn't easy.

Many times have I found it hard to keep the heart open, but such a simple thing as a dragonfly reminds me of the interconnectedness of all life, and how very precious we all are, everyone without exception. I honour my soul choice to come here by aiming to aid humanities lifting, and to complete what was not completed other times in history due to ignorance and human frailty. I will not give up until all remember how magnificent they are, just as they are without any adornment, just with love in the heart.

The Year 2012 is an eventful time – the conclusion of one era, an alignment of energies, but also the beginning of a fresh new age of discovery. A new world awaits us, one of our making, will it be we remember our divine heritage and at last begin to create heaven on earth?

It is my wish it is so.

Virginia

11 AN INVITATION

AN INVITATION TO COME HOME.

A gentle word of love heals many wounds and a heart full of pain, but this book holds the hope for the ages; a gentle message of love written by the Ascended Masters, Leonardo da Vinci, Sandro Botticelli, Isaac Newton, Martin Luther King junior, and I Lord Machiventa Melchizedek, and the Feminine Essence is represented by my partner for this writing.

Long have we urged the replenishment of love for the Sacred Feminine. Over the ages femininity has taken the brunt of man's misguided belief in his own superiority, and this illusion hasn't been aided by the misinformation given in religious teachings which propelled the image of man as conquer of the earth and all upon it.

Women, femininity has not fared well, and this is our attempt to correct this. We have issued words to aid with consciousness raising, but only one person knows the truth of these words, that truth rests in the hearts of each one of you.

You are the key to planetary growth and a new and profound wisdom and knowledge taking off to heal a world in the throes of destructive tendencies. We urge each one of you to listen to your heart, and to your own divine connection to God.

You are being summoned home! No longer do we see you blinded by ignorance and a desire to be separated from the Creator, but holding a Light all can share. Come home, back into the Sacred Heart of God. We invite you home, all who serve God choose to aid you.

See your pathway home is there, and all you need to do is love - love and take a gentle moment to connect and say, "Ah my Creator, I am here, show me my own direct connection to you, lead me, enter my life and be my strength. This is my desire to come home to you, and live with your love in my heart", and love will flood in pouring in through the heart. God is your direct heritage, you but need to invite this Divine Light in. You are divine, and so is every being on earth now - the majority have forgotten this loving connection, and have been taught that you cannot have a relationship directly, wrong! It is your divine right to do so, please remember – awaken, show others the way home, and it is through love.

The world you have entered into this incarnation is a world now struggling, and the safe route home is through love, remember that as you see others struggling and share this love with them also.

This is my invitation, come join me, join us, Christ Light is offered and given to you. We welcome you with open arms.

Be the light of understanding others need, and show them the way home by example, not pushing or preaching, just shine your divine light out, a light in the wilderness and know we are with you.

Love shows the way, and as that one who holds the Office of Christ now and in future times, I will come and welcome your home.

Profound blessings for your journey.
Lord Melchizedek.

OTHER BOOKS BY THIS AUTHOR, VRC

Deliverer Of The Light - The Soul's Journey – St Luke
ISBN 0 646 21685 6
$24.95 AUS

Between Two Worlds – St Luke @ Shamana
ISBN 0 95859530 X
$29.95 Aus

Lord Melchizedek-Transmissions of Hope –
Through Troubled Times – Volume One
ISBN 978-1463559373
$29.95 Aus

Lord Melchizedek-Transmissions of Hope –
Through Troubled Times – Volume Two
ISBN 978-0987182616
$29.95 Aus
Books are available from;

+61 2 46831581
Mobile: 0429 939181
Email: wingsinc@dodo.com.au
http://www.wingsinc.com.au/creative/shop.html
http://transmissionsofhope.com.au

 amazon.com

Coming Books:
The Sacred Feminine -
From The Feminine Aspect – Ascended Masters – & VRC
12 Journals.

www.ingramcontent.com/pod-product-compliance
Lightning Source LLC
Chambersburg PA
CBHW050341230426
43663CB00010B/1947